Planning with and for Children
UK edition

Practical guide to inquiry-based learning through Floorbooks®

Dr Claire Warden

Title:	Planning with and for Children – UK edition Practical guide to inquiry-based learning through Floorbooks®
Author:	Dr Claire Warden
Editor:	Tanya Tremewan
Designer:	Diane Williams
Book code:	TS0323
ISBN:	978-1-922530-77-6
Published:	2025
Publisher:	Teaching Solutions (Imprint of Essential Resources), Melbourne, Australia ph: 1800 005 068 ph: 0800 087 376 info@essentialresources.com.au info@essentialresources.co.nz
Website:	www.essentialresources.com.au www.essentialresources.co.nz
Copyright:	Text: © Dr Claire Warden, 2025 Edition: © Essential Resources Educational Publishers Limited, 2025 Photos: © Dr Claire Warden, 2025, with the following exceptions: pp 4, 9 (bottom left), 27, 28, 88 released into the public domain under CC0 1.0 Universal (CC0 1.0) https://creativecommons.org/publicdomain/zero/1.0/legalcode; pp 8, 54 (right, bottom), 78, 97 (right), 98 (right) © Boldon Nursery School, England; pp 17 (right), 40 (left, top and bottom), 41 © Ferntop Preschool, Tennessee, USA; pp 50 (right), 51 © Mill Hill Nursery School, England; pp 42 (right, bottom), 43, 44 (left, top), 53, 54 (top, left and right) © Nurture through Nature, WA, Australia; pp 46 (left, top), 68 (right), 69, 70, 71 (left, top and bottom) © Springdale Heights Preschool, NSW, Australia; p 49 (left, middle) © The Nature School, NSW, Australia; pp 10 (left and middle), 18–20, 22, 25, 30 (right), 31–36, 39 (right, top and bottom), 48 (right, top and bottom), 49 (left, top and bottom; right, top and bottom), 55 (right, bottom), 59 (left, top and bottom), 95 (right, bottom) © Whitefield Nursery and Infant School, England; pp 9 (right, top and bottom), 10 (right) © Woodleigh School, VIC, Australia; p 57 © KIN Nature Kindergarten, Wales; pp 60 (bottom), 61–62 © Barrhill Early Years Centre, Scotland
About the author:	Dr Claire Warden is an educational consultant with an international reputation for her pioneering work in nature pedagogy and inquiry-based learning. Her pathway to this point has included working in a range of early childhood settings and primary schools, undertaking advisory work to organisations and government and lecturing in further education. In 2010 she and her husband founded Living Classrooms, a not-for-profit organisation that supports communities through a virtual nature school.
Acknowledgements:	Thank you to all those educators who chose to stand beside me all those years ago and stand up for the right of all children to be heard. A specific thank you to the centres listed above for their images and to the following authors of the case studies: Rebekah Garwood is an early childhood consultant at the Association of Independent Schools Western Australia. She is a strong advocate for the needs and the rights of young children and enjoys supporting educators to take teaching and learning beyond the classroom walls. Erica Mason, Jenny Hutchinson and Rebecca Burns are, respectively, the headteacher and EYFS and nursery leaders at Whitefield Nursery and Infant School in Lancashire, England, a three-form entry infant school for three- to seven-year-olds. Creativity lies at the heart of the school curriculum and is used as a vehicle to develop children's language and critical thinking. (Mrs M @whitefieldhead, Jenny Hutchinson @JennyPennys and Mrs Burns @BridgeRebecca) Natashja Treveton and Nicole Halton are authors and founders of Inspired EC. They work with settings across Australia and New Zealand to develop the use of Floorbooks for documentation and planning inside and outside. Marion and Sarah Bryers are the founders of Nurture Through Nature, a nature-based early years centre in Mandurah, Western Australia for children from six weeks to six years (www.nurturethroughnature.com.au). Elizabeth McKie is a teacher in Barrhill Early Years Centre, Scotland. Funded through the local authority, the centre has a small number of children on the roll, which allows in-depth support for language development. (elizabeth.mckie4@south-ayrshire.gov.uk) Sal Preston is the founder of KIN Nature Kindergarten – the first completely outdoor setting for children aged 2–5 years in Monmouthshire, Wales. (@kids.in.nature, hello@kidsinnature.co.uk)

Copyright notice

All rights reserved. Except as permitted under the Copyright Licensing Agency (CLA) UK (for example, a fair dealing for the purposes of study, research, criticism or review), no part of this book may be reproduced, stored in a retrieval system, or transmitted in any form or by any means without prior written permission. Copyright owners may take legal action against a person or organisation who infringes their copyright through unauthorised copying. All inquiries should be directed to the publisher at the address above.

Contents

Introduction 4

Section 1. Pedagogical thinking behind Floorbooks 6
    History of Floorbooks 7
    Creating the environment 9
    Concept-led and inquiry-based play and learning 13
    Research behind the Floorbook Approach 21
    Slow learning through Floorbooks 24
    Inclusive practice 37
    Thinking about practice 40

Section 2. Features 42
    Philosophy 42
    The starting point 44
    Authorship and agency 44
    Tracking flow and progression 47
    Noticing 48
    Digital documentation 50
    Representation 52
    Community of the child, parents and educator 55
    Sharing the process of playful inquiries 58
    Reflect – looking in, out, forward and back 59
    Possible lines of development (PLODs) 60
    Demonstrating action and response 63
    The learning journey – tracking learning inside, outside and beyond 64
    Accountability for breadth and balance 64

Section 3. Key strategies 68
    Talking Tubs 68
    3D mind mapping 75
    Questioning 77

Section 4. Breadth, balance and accountability 80
    Principles that underpin curricula 80
    The planning cycle 89

Conclusion 98

References and further reading 99

Glossary 103

Introduction

Welcome to the world of inquiry-based practice through Floorbooks®. The overall aim of this book, and my work more generally, is to bring back joy to the planning process so that we engage with it with a pedagogically driven desire to understand more about what and how children think. When we understand even a small part of what children think, then we can create environments, spaces and interactions that are relevant and rich.

In this book, which links directly to the early years curricula of England and Northern Ireland, Scotland and Wales, I explore some of the foundational research that supports the use of Floorbooks before turning to all the practical elements of Floorbooks and share strategies that you can easily use to create an approach to documentation and planning that is both with and for children.

The book itself consists of four main sections:
1. pedagogical thinking behind Floorbooks
2. features of a Floorbook
3. key strategies that relate to the adult role, such as Talking Tubs
4. achieving breadth, balance and accountability.

There are images to motivate you and international case studies to inspire you. A key aspect of international writing is to find inspiration from practice in other countries as well as to acknowledge that it is place-based and affected by culture, climate and curriculum, especially when you make nature-based learning integral to your inquiries. We can all benefit from taking a fresh look at what we do and the strategies we use. In a paper on pedagogical practice, Livingston et al (2017) suggest that we look at the following aspects throughout education when evaluating our practice. All of these aspects are central to planning with and for children through Floorbooks:

- learner engagement
- mutual respect between educators and learners
- building on prior learning
- meaningful interactions
- relevance of curriculum
- developing skills and attitudes as well as knowledge
- aligning planning and assessment with the learner's needs.

INTRODUCTION

In addition, Floorbooks go further to be a vehicle to explore and make visible some of the implicit and subtle aspects of both our personal and group pedagogies, such as:

- social justice
- cultural capital
- inclusivity
- agency and empowerment
- perception of the natural world.

Floorbooks are a hub for many forms of documentation. If a setting embraces the philosophy of consultation, it will have four core strategies that work collectively to involve children, families and educators in the planning and documentation. These strategies and many more are explored in this book.

An assessment of the children is gathered through these many perspectives and used to complete a Floorbooks Planning diary, which is where the operational thoughts of the team are noted.

As we start this journey together, it is important to note that care, respect and wonderment are central traits to the role of being an adult who works with children in inquiry-based approaches. To co-construct new thinking, children and adults need to be open to creating an environment that embraces individuality within a community of practice, to be responsive and dynamic, while keeping an eye on the balance and breadth of experience.

Floorbook – used as a central location for the documentation of the process of play and the accountability to curriculum

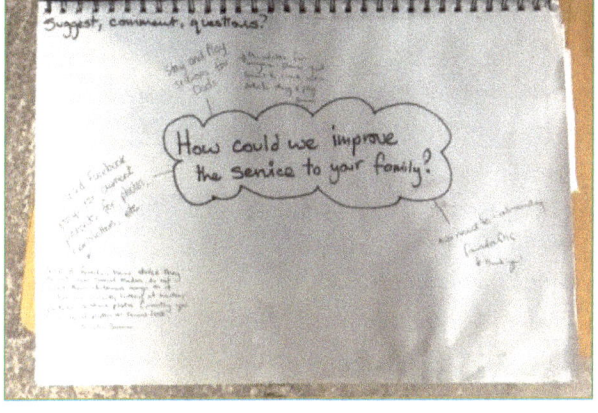

Communication Book – a shared space for the documentation of events, ideas and comments from the community

Talking Tub – a collection of fascinating, real materials to support dialogue and consultation

Portfolio or Family Book – individual learning stories in a real book for children to revisit

5

Section 1.
Pedagogical thinking behind Floorbooks

Inquiry-based learning itself has been part of an educational offering for hundreds of years as people questioned and researched the world around them. Sadly, in many countries, learning inside through direct instruction overtook a more balanced approach that had involved both teaching core skills inside and the application of those skills in real-world learning. Play moved from having freedom and autonomy to being over-controlled, as practice sought to minimise its role in education. There is currently a drive to seek that sense of balance again and to start any learning journey through consulting children to explore their fascinations, theories and plans.

These ideas become part of the planning cycle so that the decision-making power moves from being adult-only to a shared construction between children and adults. Social pedagogies tend to focus on the relationships between aspects of learning and are affected by the status each aspect is given. Any social situation involves hierarchies, which have led to an increased focus on adult-created plans for evidence and a lack of power and agency given to children. The location and use of power are at the centre of reflexive practice, which is intertwined with the reflective thinking used throughout this approach.

There are many approaches to how to teach. For me, it has been about embracing divergent thinking that supports the individual within a group-learning community. My teaching focus, in all aspects of working with people from birth to 18 years old, is to foster understanding.

Teaching for understanding

An inductive approach to how we work blends the mind and heart when exploring any curriculum. This allows us to transfer concepts to a range of new situations. This style of work takes facts or theories, looks for patterns and similarities, and then forms a generalisation with a clear indication of where it came from. An example would be to notice that a beetle sheds its case, our hair grows and a plant buds, so that we come to understand the concept of growth.

The second type of thinking is deductive reasoning, which looks at generalised truths first and then explores factual examples to validate the generalisations. An example based on the above would be to start from a statement that all things grow and then to grow sunflowers.

Both these types of teaching, which are either divergent or convergent, require us to be aware of synergistic thinking, which is the interaction between factual and conceptual levels of thinking (Erickson and Lanning 2013, p 10).

The use of inductive or open-ended teaching runs underneath many models of early education, such as those influenced by Pestalozzi, and later Malaguzzi, that appear in Reggio Emelia or those within the child-led inquiries in nature pedagogy (Warden 2018). Two main aspects of this pedagogy are of note.

First, inductive teaching, or some might suggest interaction, provides the space children need to think first and then create a learning journey that could take them inside, outside into the nature-based space and beyond the gate into the wilder spaces.

Second, when we provide the generalisation at the start of an inquiry, it affects the empowerment of children to drive it forward. If you know exactly where a journey will end, would you really be as motivated to engage in it?

Attitudes to learning – capacities of learners

Open-mindedness. Learners are supported to be open-minded in their work, and develop a growth mindset that recognises it takes time to uncover what you think may be new and different. Everyone can engage in concept-based inquiries as they focus on the relationship between the thinker and the concept itself. Where knowledge can often be portrayed as defined, concepts are

SECTION 1. PEDAGOGICAL THINKING BEHIND FLOORBOOKS

wider and free-ranging. The culture of acceptance and social justice requires children to be non-judgemental and open to their bias.

Persistent-mindedness. This attitude involves thinking that you can and believing in your internal self that you can achieve. This requires determination to persevere, to delve into the detail of a problem to find a hook that will give you a new insight. Floorbooks make this process more visible as they give the failures and challenges of learning equal status to the solutions.

Evidence-mindedness. Learners explore examples, facts and evidence before making generalised assertions or truths. Through using Floorbooks as a holder of memories, truths can be explored through experience rather than through a screen. Floorbooks often share the research alongside the children's original ideas so that both are valued.

Brain research

The field of neuroscience provides research into how the brain works that was not available at the time of many theorists such as Vygotsky or Piaget. Here are some points to consider from the research that support child-led, inquiry-based practice shared within the pages of a Floorbook.

- **Engagement.** The presence of brain research has had an impact on the commitment to active, engaging methods that foster positive dispositions to lifelong learning (Hart 1983; Howard 2006; Sylwester 1995, 2004; Zull 2002).

  There is a strong suggestion that learning dispositions are affected by emotionally led learning (Howard 2006; Wolfe 2001).

  Children's feelings about an experience affect how successful the child is in learning a skill (Sylwester 1995).

- **Interconnected thinking.** Learning is easier when experiences are interconnected rather than in isolated subject areas (Howard 2006).

- **Challenging environments.** The brain adapts and develops through continuously changing and challenging environments (Kotulak 1993).

History of Floorbooks

The use of Floorbooks started in my practice in the early 1990s. Now, after 30 years, they have stood the test of time and have international appeal across all age groups of children. My exploration of this way of working started through a postgraduate qualification in science all those years ago, where the desire to hear, to truly listen to children's ideas about the world around them, drove innovation. I selected electricity as a subject I assumed young children wouldn't know much about. How wrong I was. In the pages below we can see the opposite; given the appropriate materials to handle they were able to verbalise and demonstrate their thinking that had passed unnoticed before. Rifts in our thinking (Caputo 1987) create significant shifts in our practice – this was such a time for me and pushed me to consider aspects of empowerment, inclusivity and engagement while still being accountable to an unyielding national curriculum mandated by law.

 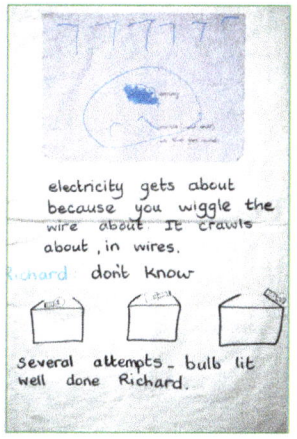

The first ever Floorbook, including cover (top) and inside pages. The diagram on the left is to share thinking about a lightbulb

SECTION 1. PEDAGOGICAL THINKING BEHIND FLOORBOOKS

In the days before digital photography, images were taken infrequently and only arrived at the setting after a delay while they were printed, so the constant fear of missing a moment was secondary to effective, caring interactions. We explore this aspect of documentation in Section 3.

A larger strategic vision is rooted in the United Nations Convention on the Rights of the Child, where articles 31 and 12 are the rights to play and to be heard. When these rights are embedded at the heart of educational pedagogy through the actual act of planning, then the values of participation, respect, empowerment and agency can flourish.

Exactly how a setting or school uses the Floorbook Approach is affected by its culture of empowerment and consultation, pedagogical principles and the impact of curriculum. The strength of a Floorbook itself lies in its flexibility, while having core features that elevate it from being a scrapbook to a Floorbook. Here are five key features that act as a foundation to start our journey into this work.

1. Floorbooks can document learning within inquiry-based projects or single aspects of learning. They provide an evidence-based log to inform tracking and demonstrate coverage of the curriculum as it documents inquiry-based learning through a lens. The adult can widen the lens to be everything children encounter, or narrow it down to exploring a fragment such as the pattern of rain on a puddle.
2. Floorbooks are used to track learning, enhance language skills and develop children's vocabulary as they use the process of recording and then sharing those opportunities, thoughts and theories back to the child in a process of metacognition.
3. They encourage a wider range of vocabulary to enrich children's language and communication skills in the broadest sense. The Talking Tub introduces objects linked to the wider project. Children ask questions about them and, if they show a particular interest in an object, the centre can note it so that it can respond through further conversation or objects to extend the idea. Floorbooks can be used to plan and record this experience.

Thinking Tree is available at all times

4. Floorbooks themselves hold so many memories of rich process-based learning that they warrant being valued and made accessible to children through the book corner. The learning journey held within them can be displayed on a wall so that parents are aware of the learning. Floorbooks can be used during parents' evenings to showcase each child's learning and encourage other adults to see the process of play through the documentation.
5. The exact type of book used as a Floorbook is secondary to its role. The A2 book has the benefit of enabling all children to access and see the pages, but the smaller A3 size is easier to move and store.

SECTION 1. PEDAGOGICAL THINKING BEHIND FLOORBOOKS

Creating the environment

To develop capacities in children, we need to create an environment that 'allows' autonomy and divergent thinking rather than a space that implicitly suggests compliance and convergent thinking.

Four types of learning environment defined by Claxton and Carr (2004) are useful to explore as they have an impact on the quality and use of the Floorbook.

First, a **prohibitive or discouraging** environment is where some activities prevent collaboration. Children follow a set, tightly packed schedule, which encourages them to see learning in little boxes. In these environments, the Floorbook becomes an evidence folder with a very high level of adult control over what is included and what is not.

The second environment is **permissive and affording**. Here resources are not easily accessible for children, value is placed on some activities but not others and teachers apply their own values rather than those of the children to the environment. In these environments, Floorbooks are well presented but only selected pieces of evidence are included.

Provide access to the Floorbook in a central area

Create environments that value dialogue for everyone in the community (above). The place of oracy in education (left)

Third is an **inviting and encouraging** environment, where working with others is actively encouraged and value is placed on the questions that children ask. Activities are available but choice is still limited. Here we can see that children's voices are valued and included through the child writing and drawing, and the process of play is valued and shared through film and audio.

9

SECTION 1. PEDAGOGICAL THINKING BEHIND FLOORBOOKS

In the fourth **expansive, powerful and potentiating** environment, the experiences that emerge from the planning in Floorbooks are elevated and engaged with every day. Here teachers supply the tools and resources but allow the children to make the decisions about what and how they learn. Children frequently participate in shared activities where they can develop their learning dispositions. In these environments the Floorbook runs alongside the inquiry, holding memories and ideas of a community of play within the setting.

Inspiring talk

Making portfolios accessible to children and families

SECTION 1. PEDAGOGICAL THINKING BEHIND FLOORBOOKS

England and Northern Ireland

The Early Years Foundation Stage (EYFS) is a guidance framework that became statutory in September 2021. The 'early years' covers children from birth to five years old.

The Northern Ireland curriculum and the English curriculum are linked through their use of the EYFS framework.

This statutory framework is for school leaders, school staff, childcare providers, childminders and out-of-school providers.

The EYFS sets the standards that all early years providers must meet so that children learn and develop well and are kept healthy and safe. It promotes teaching and learning to develop children's 'school readiness' and gives children the broad range of knowledge and skills that will establish the foundation they need to progress well through school and life in the future.

The EYFS seeks to provide:
- quality and consistency in all early years settings, so that every child makes good progress and no child gets left behind
- a secure foundation through planning for the learning and development of each individual child, and regularly assessing and reviewing what they have learnt
- partnerships between practitioners, as well as for practitioners working with parents and carers
- equality of opportunity and anti-discriminatory practice, so that every child is included and supported.

The EYFS specifies requirements for learning and development and for safeguarding children and promoting their welfare. The learning and development requirements cover:
- the areas of learning and development that must shape activities and experiences (educational programmes) for children in all early years settings
- the early learning goals that providers must help children work towards (the knowledge, skills and understanding children should have at the end of the academic year in which they turn five)
- assessment arrangements for measuring progress (and requirements for reporting to parents and carers). (Department for Education, England 2025)

Scotland

A number of documents influence the quality of early education in Scotland. Alongside regional guidance, national documents that play a part are:
- *Realising the Ambition – Being Me* (Education Scotland 2020)
- refreshed narrative on Scotland's Curriculum for Excellence (Education Scotland 2019)
- *Health and Social Care standards – My support, My life* (Scottish Government 2017)
- *A Quality Improvement Framework for the Early Learning and Childcare Sectors* (Education Scotland and Care Inspectorate 2025)
- *How Good Is Our Early Learning and Childcare?* (Education Scotland 2016).

continued ...

SECTION 1. PEDAGOGICAL THINKING BEHIND FLOORBOOKS

In all of these documents, children have the right to be valued as active learners who choose, plan and challenge themselves. This stimulates a climate of reciprocity, 'listening' to children (even if they cannot speak), observing how their feelings, curiosity, interest and knowledge are engaged in their early childhood environments, and encouraging them to contribute to their own learning (Smith 2007). This starting point for planning builds a community of practitioners and family that supports and extends the open-ended nature of playful inquiries.

In the early stages of schooling, Scottish curriculum documents encourage integrating inquiry with learning. However, a pedagogical shift is involved in moving from direct teaching to embracing teaching as inquiry. Timperley and colleagues (2014, p 22) suggest that 'it is not a project, an initiative or an innovation but a professional way of being'.

Realising the Ambition – Being Me reflects the original principles and philosophy of an earlier document, *Building the Ambition*, and complements the current policy direction of early learning and childcare (ELC) and early primary education towards play-based pedagogies. It aspires to support practitioners in delivering what babies, toddlers and young children need most and how practitioners can deliver this most effectively in Scotland to give children the best start in life (Education Scotland 2020, p 10).

The Scottish curriculum documents view planning as responsive, interwoven with intentional interactions. As Floorbooks are built on the concept of working in the moment, they support practitioners to take a planning approach that they do with and for children so that the interactions, experiences and spaces either change or stay the same in ways that best meet their needs.

Wales

The Curriculum for Wales provides an integrated framework to support adults to bring together the six areas of: expressive arts; health and well-being; humanities; languages, literacy and communication; mathematics and numeracy; and science and technology.

The six areas bring together familiar disciplines and encourage strong and meaningful links across them. The individual disciplines still play an important role, especially as learners progress and begin to specialise.

The Curriculum for Wales guidance (Welsh Government 2024) promotes collaboration and cross-disciplinary planning, learning and teaching, both within and across areas. This will enable learners to build connections across their learning and combine different experiences, knowledge and skills.

Enabling Pathways focuses on the following aspects as fundamental to successful pedagogy:
- play and playful learning
- being outdoors
- observation
- authentic and purposeful learning.

In all of these aspects, children have the right to be valued as active learners who choose, plan, and challenge themselves. This stimulates a climate of reciprocity, 'listening' to children (even if

continued ...

they cannot speak), observing how their feelings, curiosity, interest and knowledge are engaged in their early childhood environments, and encouraging them to contribute to their own learning (Smith 2007). When this is the starting point for planning, it builds a community of educators and families that supports and extends the open-ended nature of playful inquiries.

In the early stages of school, the curriculum encourages the integration of inquiry. However, a pedagogical shift occurs from direct teaching to embracing teaching as inquiry. Timperley and colleagues (2014, p 22) suggest that 'it is not a project, an initiative or an innovation but a professional way of being'.

Concept-led and inquiry-based play and learning

Anybody who is fascinated by the questions of *Who? What? Why? When? How?* is an inquirer. Having a desire to widen your horizon for no other reason than that desire points to a growth mindset to uncover new thinking and perspectives. Inquiry-based learning has been used as a term since the 1960s, when it was often linked to science-based learning; however, the pedagogy is transferable across all areas of learning.

Each of the four kinds of inquiry-based learning is suited to particular types of classrooms. They comprise the following, ordered here from most to least structured.

- **Confirmation inquiry.** You give children a question, its answer and the method of reaching this answer. Their goal is to build investigation and critical thinking skills, learning how the specific method works.
- **Structured inquiry.** You give children an open question and an investigation method. They must use the method to craft an evidence-backed conclusion.
- **Guided inquiry.** You give children an open question. Typically in groups, they then design investigation methods to reach a conclusion.
- **Open inquiry.** You give children time and support. They pose original questions that they investigate through their own methods and eventually present their results to discuss and expand.

Inquiry-based pedagogies support all aspects of the curriculum in a holistic way. These inquiries include traditionally separate curriculum areas, attitudes or dispositions and skills. With language skills, for example, we explore the five aspects described on the following page when we use a Floorbook and a Talking Tub. Given that language moves across curricular divisions, it has a holistic impact on a young child's growth and development.

Example: Exploring language skills with a Floorbook and Talking Tub

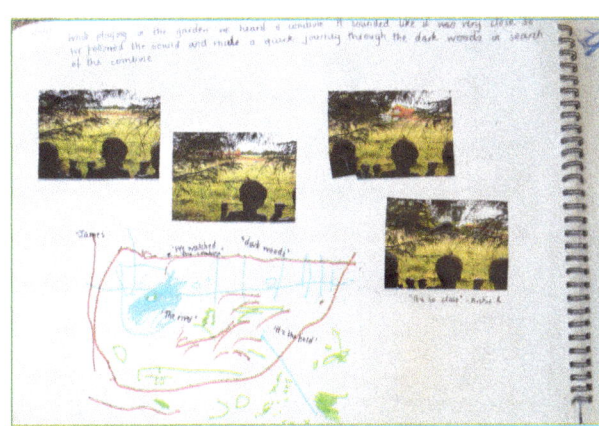

Gathering information from experiences

SECTION 1. PEDAGOGICAL THINKING BEHIND FLOORBOOKS

Information processing skills

- Gather information from people and through texts and images in the Talking Tub.
- Analyse and compare 2D and 3D objects.
- Sequence memory, objects and images.
- Classify and sort found materials and focus objects in the Talking Tub.

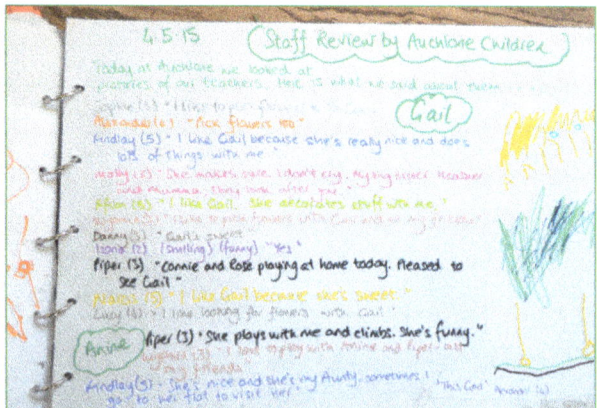

Discussion for a staff review

Evaluation skills

- Evaluate options through discussion.
- Monitor progress through a learning journey mind map either in the Floorbook or on a wall-based version.
- Reflect on one's own and others' progress through revisiting Floorbooks and Family Books.

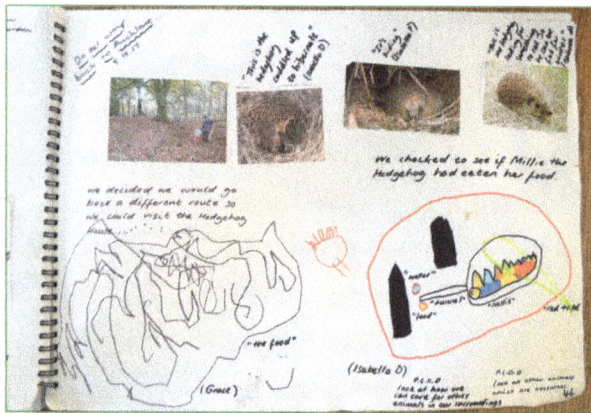

Documentation of decision-making

Reasoning skills

- Make informed decisions when exploring the complexity of the Talking Tub.
- Arrive at group-reasons for choices, with these recorded as voting or meeting notes.

- Make inferences and connections as they revisit moments through the Floorbook.
- Make deductions as they consider the process, complete with failures and successes.

Mathematical problem-solving between home and setting

Inquiry skills

- Plan what, where, when and how.
- Test ideas and explore why things happen as they do.
- Predict experiences and understand cause and effect.
- Solve problems through real-world experiences that are then documented to aid recall.

Real-world and core skills come together in construction inquiry

Creative skills

- Apply imagination through divergent thinking.
- Look for alternatives and options.
- Generate ideas through dialogue with others.
- Vocalise possibilities for learning in partnership with adults.

Some children appear to complete tasks to gain positive feedback from an adult or to avoid failure. For this reason, Bruner (1961) suggested that such children may not appreciate the inherent benefits of experiencing failure in the learning process.

When the inquiry-based approach is linked to using Floorbooks as a planning tool, children develop a growth mindset rather than a fixed mindset. This happens because a Floorbook shares the process of discovery and failure and makes visible that there are multiple ways of responding to one idea. Because of this, children grow to enjoy the learning process itself and learn to love it in itself, rather than just feeling rewarded by the approval and praise of a parent or teacher.

Viewing inquiry-based learning from the two different perspectives of a child and an educator allows us to usefully consider its point of difference from other, more directional approaches to educating children.

- **From a child's point of view**, inquiry-based play is offered in an open but well-thought-through environment that allows them to test, explore and investigate how the world works. They feel that they have the power to make decisions and choices.

- **From an educator's perspective**, inquiry-based play supports children's curiosity as this stimulates increased activity in the hippocampus, the region of the brain responsible for memory creation (von Stumm et al 2011). This moves children's thinking into the realms of deeper understanding by slowing down the content *you think you should cover* to focus on learning skills, forming attitudes and developing capacity through the contexts that fascinate them.

The nature of concept-led inquiry

A concept-led inquiry is broader than a defined subject such as 'animals'. This kind of inquiry considers relational concepts, such as growth, change and transformation, and how those concepts are present in a wide range of real-world contexts. So, for example, we could look at the growth of a dog, but we could also look at growth in a human or indeed a salt crystal or a plant. This focus on the underlying relationships supports children to see patterns and connections in learning that are not always obvious in other approaches. Everywhere in the world are people who think deeply about how we are educating our children. As an educational innovator, my work sometimes resides on the periphery of a standardised educational system, as it promotes a divergent way of thinking, which can be at odds with systems designed to define and measure children.

Of course, this work has bridges and connections as well as a measure of flexibility. A little consultation is better than none and small steps in this work can build to create social change, as we have seen in the growth of nature-based pedagogies, where documentation has allowed the decision-makers to access the incredible complexity of thinking involved.

I seek to move beyond memorising facts, to seeing concepts, patterns and relationships in the world. The status and balance given to knowledge, skills and concepts come through in forming the curriculum and its delivery through models of education and their associated pedagogy of the what, where and how of teaching and learning.

We know that the idea of children exploring their own questions and theories is present in varying degrees around the world. It may be useful to consider the phases of concept-based inquiry, such as those presented by French and Marschall (2016, p 29). Table 1.1 offers an overview of these phases. I develop this discussion further in Section 4 in relation to planning diaries.

Table 1.1: Phases of concept-based inquiry

Phase	Purpose
Engage	- To engage children emotionally and intellectually in the inquiry. - To activate and assess children's prior knowledge. - To invite initial questions.
Focus	- To introduce relevant factual examples that may be explored further in the 'investigate' phase of an inquiry. - To consider all forms of language skills and which ones may be more relevant to this particular inquiry.
Investigate	- To explore factual examples, or case studies, and connect these to unit concepts. - To expand students' understanding of unit concepts by providing case studies that introduce complexity and/or raise additional questions. - To acquire disciplinary and interdisciplinary skills.
Organise	- To organise thinking at both factual and conceptual levels. - To represent concepts and ideas using different materials or media, and/or subject areas for older children. - To recognise and analyse skills in context.
Generalise	- To form connections and locate patterns across factual examples. - To articulate, justify and communicate generalisations.
Transfer (beyond the inquiry)	- To test and justify the validity of generalisations. - To apply generalisations to new events and situations. - To use experiences and understandings to form predictions and hypotheses.
Reflect (through all phases of the inquiry)	- To build students' sense of personal agency. - To enable students to plan and monitor their learning process. - To individually and collectively evaluate learning progress during and at the end of an inquiry.

These phases are cyclical rather than linear. We know that inquiries are complex and random for a reason, as they allow lines of inquiry to overlap and move around to follow a range of learning journeys. In Section 2, I present strategies used in the Floorbooks as a toolkit, so that educators have the freedom to use any one of them when they feel it is most appropriate. The flow of the Floorbook runs over many weeks or months, and is revisited several times a week to maintain the connection with children. By using the analogy of a river with this approach, we can visualise what is happening over the lifetime of a Floorbook, as I describe in more detail in Section 4. If we superimpose the cyclical nature of playful inquiries on the surface of the river, they would appear like spirals of current rising through the river as moments emerge, are experienced and let go while the larger journey of inquiry keeps moving forward.

Project-based learning

Project-based learning is an in-depth study, over an extended period, of a topic that is of high interest to an individual, a small group or a whole class (Helm and Katz 2001). Children learn skills and concepts through their inquiries that are co-created with adults. This approach is similar to thematic investigations but differs in its emphasis on a child-driven focus to the inquiry. Popular in the USA, this approach has enabled settings to meet the demands of set curricula while also embracing children's fascinations. Documentation is shared in a variety of ways, such as with a Learning Wall that develops over time.

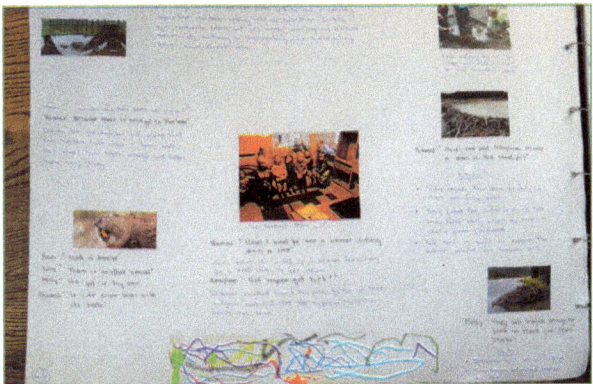

Children as researchers

Pedagogical documentation and inspiration from the preschools of Reggio Emilia

Documentation in Reggio Emilia preschools has several functions. Gandini (1993, p 8) suggests that these are to:

- make parents aware of their children's experiences and maintain parental involvement
- allow teachers to understand children better
- evaluate the teachers' own work, thus promoting their professional growth
- facilitate communication and exchange of ideas among educators
- make children aware that their effort is valued
- create an archive that traces the history of the school and of the pleasure and process of learning by many children and their teachers.

These points are similar to the wider work on project-based or inquiry-based learning. However, Loris Malaguzzi (1993) acknowledges that the schools of Reggio Emelia:

> have no planned curriculum with units and sub-units … instead every year each school delineates a series of related projects, some short-range and some long. These themes serve as the main structural supports but then it is up to the children. (p 87)

Sharing process in displays

It is in this area that we can observe the greatest tension for teachers in the early years and primary sectors. Several aspects of education in this area, which vary across age groups and between countries, are:

- the demand for accountability to a defined, standardised curriculum
- the high mobility of staff, especially in the early years, which has an adverse impact on consistent pedagogy
- the diversity and number of languages spoken in settings, which offer code-switching challenges for in-depth dialogue
- the impact of increasing poverty on engagement (Helm and Beneke 2003).

The point of difference between the Reggio Emelia approaches noted above and the use of Floorbooks is that Floorbooks can bridge practice from early years through into primary schools. They support high levels of pedagogical understanding, with clear meaningful contexts, and are therefore used very successfully in areas of significant deprivation due to their use in combination with the Talking Tub to support oracy, code-switching and increased cultural capital.

Case study: Mathematical thinking

by Jenny Hutchinson (UK)

This case study is framed by using questions to guide practitioners in their responses. Floorbooks and individual portfolios are used to share children's thinking.

Context: Child C accessed resources within the maths area of the classroom. She initiated play with another child and asked her peer to pass her the 'counters'. Child C then began to use the available resources to orally recount several dinosaur figures '1, 2, 3, 4, 5, 6, 7, 8 …'. Child C then repeated this activity and accurately applied her 1:1 correspondence counting skills using other available resources. The practitioner quickly enhanced Child C's mathematical thinking by prompting her to represent the value of each set of counters that she had just sequenced. Child C represented each dinosaur counter by drawing the same amount of flowers.

The practitioner then enhanced Child C's play by introducing the new concept of 'subitising'. Recognising Child C's cardinality, and ability to rapidly and accurately make judgements on the number of items or elements that needed to be enumerated, the practitioner explored and encouraged her 'number sense'. The practitioner asked Child C to think of different ways of making a number.

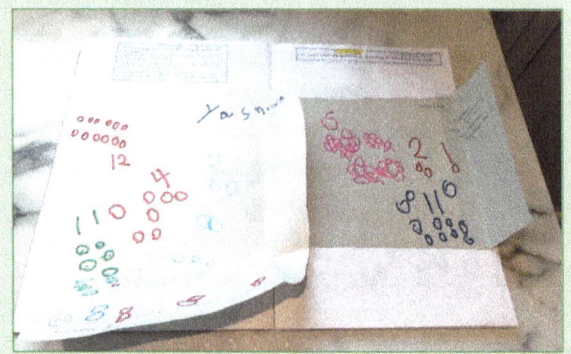

Counting dinosaurs and other objects, with children's understanding recorded in Floorbook (top right)

Documenting mathematical recordings

Child C's mathematical recordings and jottings were instantaneously exhibited on the class's 'Maths in action' display board. Child C's learning was celebrated immediately, which subsequently encouraged her to explore mathematical concepts further within the continuous provision.

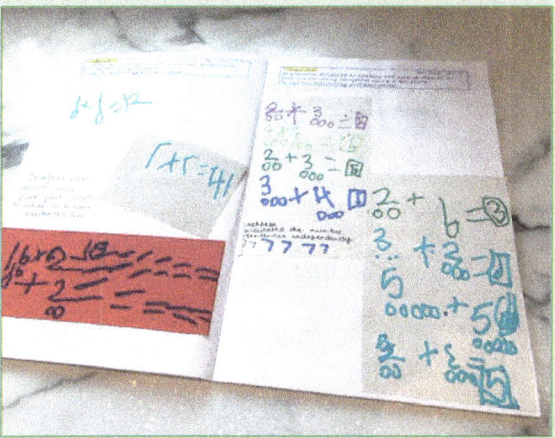

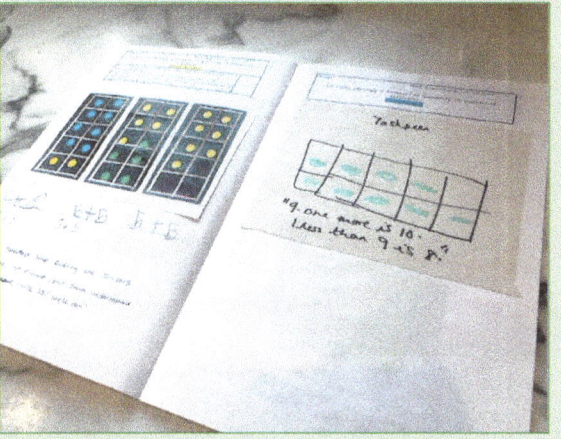

Sharing the process of mathematical thinking in wall displays (left) and a Floorbook (above)

Further developing mathematical concepts

Once Child C was fully confident in representing the value of numerals in a variety of ways and applying subitising concepts, and had a developing and accurate perspective of number sense, the practitioner introduced the 'part, part, whole' model – combining two sets of objects to find the total. The practitioner encouraged the child to arrange her counters into 'subgroups' – for example, 2 and 3, to come to the total of 5. The practitioner then asked the child to place the counters in a linear arrangement and probed the child to explore the arrangement further, starting to explore concepts such as 'greater' and 'fewer'. Recordings and jottings were displayed in Child C's workbook.

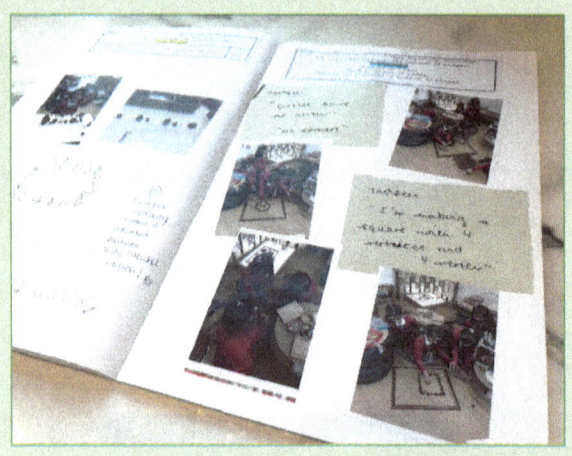

Developing more mathematical concepts or skills after Child C's journey was documented

After exploring a series of mathematical concepts such as counting linear and non-linear arrangements, subitising, cardinality, practical addition, number sequence and a whole 'sense of 10', Child C passed her knowledge on to other children in the classroom. With her newfound confidence and skills, she also explored shapes in her environment.

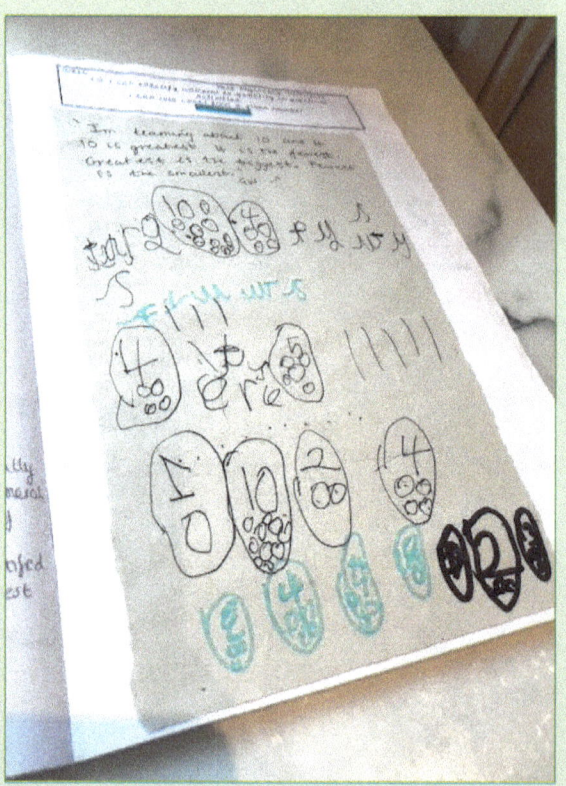

Floorbooks collated children's ideas and theories on any aspect of the curriculum

After adult input, Child C investigated patterns and shapes within her environment using natural materials. A group of peers who she gathered together began forming 2D and 3D shapes and explored new vocabulary such as *vertex* and *vertices*. From this we could record further mathematical jottings on to our 'Maths in Action' instant display.

Floorbooks can act as a hub for many forms of documentation when in the hands of children and adults as a working document and can include a range of responses. They can represent all stages of the planning cycle, from initial ideas, to observation and analysis, to intentional action, as well as the accountability to a curriculum to monitor breadth and balance.

Characteristics and benefits of inquiry-based approaches

All these playful, inquiry-based approaches have characteristics in common.

- Learning is essentially child-centred, with an emphasis on the co-construction of new knowledge and concepts.
- Adults become facilitators, providing encouragement and support to enable the students to take responsibility for what and how they learn.
- Children reach a point where they are not simply investigating questions posed by others but can formulate their own research ideas and convert that research into knowledge that they recall more effectively and consistently.
- Children gain not only a deeper understanding of the subject matter, but also the knowledge development and leadership skills required for tackling complex problems that occur in the real world.

These characteristics in turn deliver similar benefits.

- Fundamentally, children are more engaged with the subject. They perceive learning as more relevant to their own needs, thus they are enthusiastic and ready to learn.
- Children can expand on what they have learned by following their own research interests.
- Inquiry-based learning allows children to develop a more flexible approach to their studies, giving them the freedom and the responsibility to organise their own pattern of work within the time constraints of the task.

Research behind the Floorbook Approach

As they have benefits for many aspects of child development, the Floorbooks can potentially draw on many fields of research, from the benefits of agency and empowerment to the development of language. Many research evaluations have asked educators what difference they felt Floorbooks had made to their practice. These are some of their responses:

'Increased time listening to what children think.'

'When inspectors [of education] came in and loved it, I knew it was a way to be accountable but still be child-led in what we plan to do and what we document.'

'More enjoyment of the planning process.'

'An exciting way to deliver a rather dry curriculum.'

'Greater democratic decision-making, both in early years and primary school.'

'Increased engagement of adults and children in not only language but all areas of learning.'

' Parents love them; when they look at them they say ... "look that's Jonah and yes he would say that. That is so what he does".'

'Joyful times to re-read the Floorbooks with children, where they laughed at what they were doing when they were young.'

'I am an ESL teacher and the Floorbooks have revolutionised how we work. Rather than games, we use the Talking Tub for language development as it is so inclusive for my children and they feel part of the community of the setting.'

Sharing images of display in the Floorbooks

SECTION 1. PEDAGOGICAL THINKING BEHIND FLOORBOOKS

To be transparent in this research, we need to embrace the reality that some challenges are associated with using Floorbooks, as these responses capture:

'It was tricky to balance the needs of external demands for dry, very specific reporting and the joy of the Floorbook.'

'The cost of printing photos has been a barrier.'

'I struggled to fit time into a busy day to do the Floorbook and then I realised that the Floorbook is all about the day!'

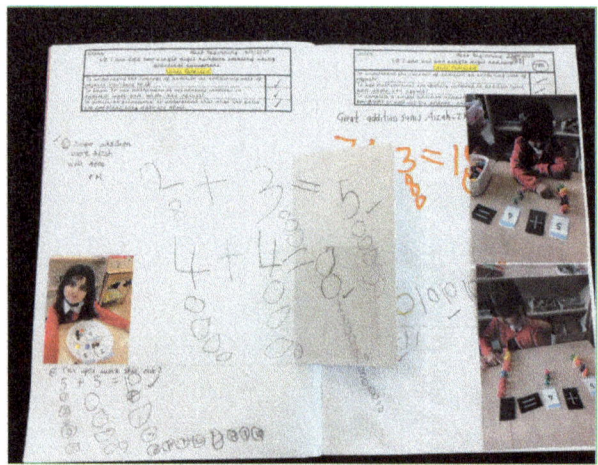

Sharing mathematical thinking as individuals

This educator research is powerful, especially when it is combined with the body of peer-reviewed research that aligns with this work. Significant examples include habits of mind (Costa and Kallick 2000), learning power (Claxton 2002) and learning orientation (Dweck 2006), which have all influenced my recent work to theorise and explain the effectiveness of the Floorbook Approach.

In his work on mathematics, Wagner (2014) discusses the idea of the transfer of pieces. If children can join the dots to see the evolution of an idea, and adults are encouraged to notice how the bits all fit together, then we can document individual progression of the same big ideas or lines of inquiry as they emerge and submerge in the learning journey. Floorbooks document all the pieces of the journey to allow children, family and educators to see the patterns in that learning journey.

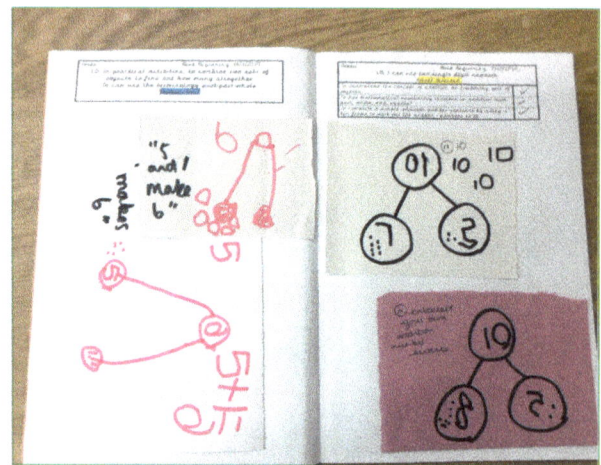

Sharing computation in a Learning Journal

The concept of thinking and researching across scales of time (Lemke 2000) encourages us to consider the length of time we document. Is the experience we focus on long enough to show progression in a learning disposition or is it just a spot in time? Lemke suggests that we use representative time scales in education for lengths of engagement, such as an utterance (one 10-second period), an exchange (seconds to minutes), an episode (about 15 minutes), a lesson (an hour), a school day, a term, a year and up to a planetary change of 3.2 billion years. In doing so we can begin to understand that learning is not a spot in time but the celebration of a journey. Floorbooks act as a holder of memories and as such can be used to recall information after a day, week, several months or even a year. When the Floorbooks are centrally held in a library area, they allow years of reference and reflection for groups of children.

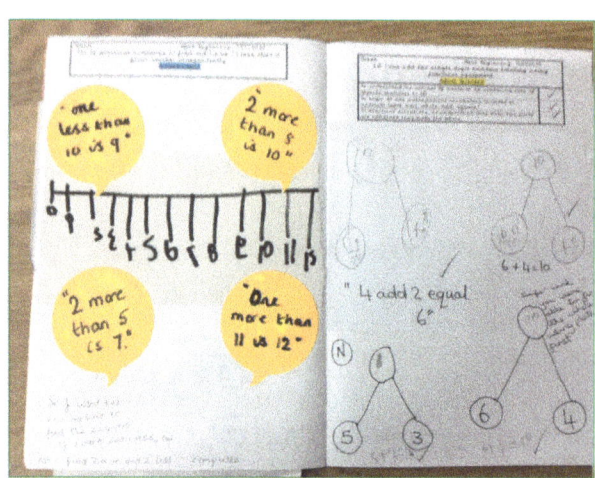

Accountability to children's thinking and to learning outcomes

SECTION 1. PEDAGOGICAL THINKING BEHIND FLOORBOOKS

The joint attention of an adult and child working together is 'an encounter between two individuals in which participants pay joint attention to, and jointly act on some external topic' (Schaffer 1996, p 101). It is well established in research that joint attention is a key element in early learning contexts and experiences during early childhood (Bruner 1996; Schaffer 1996; White et al 1979) and was included in the Effective Provision of Preschool Education (EPPE) study in England (Sylva et al 1999). This led to sustained, shared thinking with subcategories of adult-initiated and child-initiated experiences (Siraj-Blatchford and Manni 2008). In that particular research, sustained, shared thinking 'came to be defined as an effective pedagogic interaction, where two or more individuals work together in an intellectual way to solve a problem, clarify a concept, evaluate activities or extend a narrative' (p 7).

In our nature-based provision at Auchlone Nature Kindergarten in Scotland, we also see this engagement with natural materials, especially when we are in the wilder spaces around the site. If some element of these can be captured in imagery or materially, we observe a difference in the children's engagement and desire to communicate their stories and theories.

Some traces of these adventures are shared in the Floorbook and incorporated into the Talking Tubs that are then used at Talkaround Time. This engagement encourages sustained, shared thinking through framing the conversation to focus on contextual concepts, skills, attitudes and knowledge using real objects and imagery. This open-ended nature of engagement cannot be scheduled but operates as a collection of diverse experiences that all connect and mesh together through childhood.

The rejection of stages of development as a normative pathway of learning is in part due to reflective practice but also due to the research that suggests that rather than a hierarchical list we should look at alternatives (Morss 1996) or a dictionary of experiences (Rinaldi 2006, p 76) that help children to reflect, infer, hypothesise and understand. Papert (1993) further asserts that society 'has a perverse commitment to moving as quickly as possible from the concrete to the

Material traces of adventure

abstract' (p 151). As such, we push children to move away from relational real-world learning to learning that is reduced to segments and outcomes.

Relational and social theory of learning situates the learning in a context. The learning 'is not separated from the world of action but exists in robust, complex, social environments made up of actors, actions and situations' (Pitri 2004, p 6). The relationships that we create together are created in the dialogic space between the learner and the context; we 'live in the middle' (Wertsch 1998). This space allows us to focus on the actions mediated by people, places and things around us that make relationships. This middle space is well represented in Floorbooks as they hold the traces of many relationships, the sun and the shadow, the sand and the foot, as well as the relationships between humans. 'The middle is the relating; the recognising, adapting, editing, recontextualising, improvising, constructing, enjoying, puzzling about, and taking up of (or ignoring of) opportunities in the environment' (Carr 2000, p 7).

SECTION 1. PEDAGOGICAL THINKING BEHIND FLOORBOOKS

In Section 2, we return to modes of representation, but at this point let us consider what Bruner (1996) wrote in the revision of his 1971 work on three stages of representation:

> You represented the world in action routines, in pictures or in symbols and the more mature you became, the more likely you were to favour the end of the progression than the start. At the time we thought that the course from enactive through icons to symbolic representation was a progression, although I no longer think so. But I do find it useful to make a three-fold distinction in modes of representation, although not on developmental grounds. (p 155)

Floorbooks contain evidence of social change in action. They both are supported by published research – on language acquisition, motivation, engagement and learning theories through inquiry – and support educator research, as we explore in the following sections.

Slow learning through Floorbooks

When I started to use Floorbooks in 1986, I was fascinated by the lack of real-world contexts for spoken and written language in education. Floorbooks arose from a real desire to support children to engage in the classroom, but also to share their ideas and the physicality of their inquiries through talking, listening, reading and writing. The broad scope of the words embraces many ways of knowing, as you will see from the discussion of representation in Section 2, and yet the focus then, as it is now, appears to be on reducing the wonderful process of uncovering and inquiry to simple tasks and on considering that all you need to do to write is to practise handwriting. Surely there needs to be a drive and passion to connect, to share thinking and ideas, to collaborate and learn from and with each other.

Oracy

Oracy can be seen as an outcome: children learn to talk confidently, appropriately and sensitively. Floorbooks are built on the alternative view of oracy as a process, during which children learn through talk, deepening their understanding through dialogue with their teachers and peers (Alexander 2012). Oracy involves adults and children thinking carefully and deliberately about the sorts of spoken language they are using, which will vary across subjects and with different age groups. Different types of talk will be appropriate at different points in the learning cycle. Robin Alexander (2008) outlines five key types of 'teaching talk':

1. **rote:** imparting knowledge by getting children to repeat key pieces of information to tell facts, ideas and routines, such as by using 'rhymes and songs'

2. **recitation:** using questions to test children's knowledge and understanding, check their progress and stimulate recall

Journeys are documented into Floorbooks (left). Looking back at Floorbooks (above)

3. **instruction:** telling children what to do and explaining key facts, principles or processes in order to transmit information, such as 'put your hat on because it's sunny'

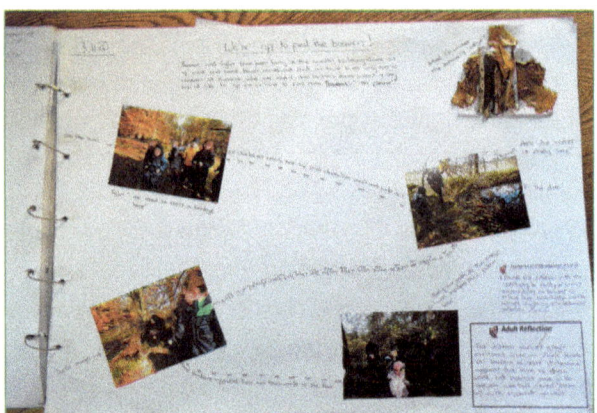

4. **discussion:** encouraging the exchange of ideas within a class, to share information

5. **dialogue:** using structured questions and discussion, which helps students deepen their understanding of key knowledge, principles and processes.

Developing and using oracy and communication in its wider definition is at the core of being heard and developing a sense of agency. Too often children are pushed through the development of oracy and into writing as a form of communication; even then, writing can be seen as an outcome or a process.

Revisiting

Modelling curiosity

Oracy in England and Northern Ireland

The development of children's spoken language underpins all seven areas of learning and development. Children's back-and-forth interactions from an early age form the foundations for language and cognitive development. Crucial factors in this development are both the number and the quality of the conversations they have with adults and peers throughout the day in a language-rich environment.

By commenting on what children are interested in or doing, echoing back what they say and adding new vocabulary, practitioners build children's language effectively. We give children the opportunity to thrive by reading frequently to them and engaging them actively in stories, non-fiction, rhymes and poems, and then providing them with extensive opportunities to use and embed new words in a range of contexts. Through conversation, storytelling and role play, during which children share their ideas with support and modelling from their teacher, and sensitive questioning that invites them to elaborate, children become comfortable with using a rich range of vocabulary and language structures (see page 8 of this book).

continued ...

SECTION 1. PEDAGOGICAL THINKING BEHIND FLOORBOOKS

Given they are books, Floorbooks create a vehicle in themselves to celebrate literacy in its widest sense. As a hub of documentation, they can show interactive, process-led learning walls, play diaries, traces of writing from children's play and, of course, conversation. The Talking Tub is designed to enrich and extend vocabulary. Given the strong context it provides, it is especially effective for children with English as a second language and those with special educational rights.

Adult-directed contexts may not match what children know and want to explore. Children's ideas and theories are the foundation for the learning journey to take place. Floorbooks provide a middle ground for a dialogue through which adults' intention and the children's plans coalesce.

The learning journey in the Floorbook makes the complex and often multidirectional way children's thinking develops visible to the team and to visitors to the setting. Literacy develops in environments rich in talk where the adults focus on the world around them so that children can share their perspectives developed from experience.

Early learning goals: Listening, attention and understanding

Children at the expected level of development will:

- listen attentively and respond to what they hear with relevant questions, comments and actions when an adult is reading to them and during whole-class discussions and small-group interactions
- make comments about what they have heard and ask questions to clarify their understanding
- hold conversation in back-and-forth exchanges with their teacher and peers.

Early learning goals: Speaking

Children at the expected level of development will:

- participate in small-group, class and one-to-one discussions, offering their own ideas and using recently introduced vocabulary
- offer explanations for why things might happen, making use of recently introduced vocabulary from stories, non-fiction, rhymes and poems when appropriate
- express their ideas and feelings about their experiences using full sentences, which can feature past, present and future tenses and conjunctions, with modelling and support from their teacher.

Because Floorbooks hold memories of process that are rich in vocabulary and meaning for children, they are an authentic way of demonstrating how children work towards and achieve the goals above. Children themselves often revisit the documentation during the day and in this social context co-construct deeper knowledge. They have space to write in Floorbooks and use the process of writing in all its forms as a way of learning.

Vital knowledge comes from rich dialogue and conversation. Engaging in conversation is actually a complex skill to learn. We need to be aware of cultural nuances in dialogue between adults and children as these affect the way children engage in group sessions and individual interactions.

SECTION 1. PEDAGOGICAL THINKING BEHIND FLOORBOOKS

Oracy in Scotland

Realising the Ambition – Being Me is not a rigid curriculum. It is concerned with experiences and outcomes that emphasise responsiveness and the child's right to drive their own learning. It states:

> Literacy, numeracy and mathematical thinking are woven within the fabric of all conversations, interactions and experiences. They are everywhere in the environment. They are part of a child's everyday life and are fundamental to all other learning. (Education Scotland 2020, p 70)

It has four overarching themes for literacy:

> Literacy can be attached to everyday learning experiences and opportunities

> Warm nurturing relationships help open up communication and connect literacy to the child's life

> Literacy experiences should weave, build and grow children's interests, vocabulary and knowledge

> Literacy learning should encourage children to see themselves as readers and writers, through purposeful experiences which build on the way that children use literacy (Education Scotland 2020, p 72)

Given they are books, Floorbooks create a vehicle in themselves to celebrate literacy in its widest sense. As a hub of documentation, they can show interactive, process-led learning walls, play diaries, traces of writing from children's play and, of course, conversation.

Adult-directed contexts may not match what children know and want to explore. Children's ideas and theories are the foundation for the learning journey to take place. Floorbooks provide a middle ground for a dialogue through which adults' intention and the children's plans coalesce.

Floorbooks hold memories of process that are rich in vocabulary and meaning for children. Children themselves often revisit the documentation during the day and in this social context co-construct deeper knowledge. They have space to write in Floorbooks and use the process of writing in all its forms as a way of learning.

Literacy experiences can be attached to everyday learning experiences and opportunities (Education Scotland 2020)

Vital knowledge comes from rich dialogue and conversation. Engaging in conversation is actually a complex skill to learn. We need to be aware of cultural nuances in dialogue between adults and children as these affect the way children engage in group sessions and individual interactions.

Oracy in Wales

The speaking of Welsh has been embedded in the curriculum and the way it is delivered over the years. Given they are books, Floorbooks create a vehicle in themselves to celebrate literacy in its widest sense. As a hub of documentation, they can show interactive, process-led learning walls, play diaries, traces of writing from children's play and, of course, conversation.

Adult-directed contexts may not match what children know and want to explore. Children's ideas and theories are the foundation for the learning journey to take place. Floorbooks provide a middle ground for a dialogue through which adults' intention and the children's plans coalesce.

The learning journey in the Floorbook makes the complex and often multidirectional way children's thinking develops visible to the team and to visitors to the setting.

Floorbooks hold memories of process that are rich in vocabulary and meaning for children. Children themselves often revisit the documentation during the day and in this social context co-construct deeper knowledge. They have space to write in Floorbooks and use the process of writing in all its forms as a way of learning.

Vital knowledge comes from rich dialogue and conversation. Engaging in conversation is actually a complex skill to learn. We need to be aware of cultural nuances in dialogue between adults and children as these affect the way children engage in group sessions and individual interactions.

Cultural nuances in children's dialogue with adults affect their engagement

SECTION 1. PEDAGOGICAL THINKING BEHIND FLOORBOOKS

Write to learn – and learn to write

As the preceding pages note, although it may seem obvious, Floorbooks are books! These giant floor-based books invite children to be the co-authors throughout the learning journey. My pedagogy embraces the emergence of skill, and that extends to writing. Floorbooks are not purely about the secretarial skills of handwriting and spelling; they embrace emergent writing. 'Emergent writing', which is synonymous with have-a-go writing and developmental writing, reflects the sequence of awareness of shape and form in scripts. It enables children to *write and be writers* as soon as they make marks on the page. The level of clarity and shared understanding of their marks develops over time.

With an increasing emphasis on the core skill of writing in the early stages, I have taken the opportunity to focus on this one aspect of Floorbooks to demonstrate the tension between the more formalised expectations of core skills and the home experience of writing and mark-making in general.

Let us consider a few of the ways in which we used writing at home in my childhood. This handwritten experience has been superseded by typing on a screen or taking an image. So where has the purpose of learning to write by hand gone and what is the impact of that?

Children writing in a Floorbook

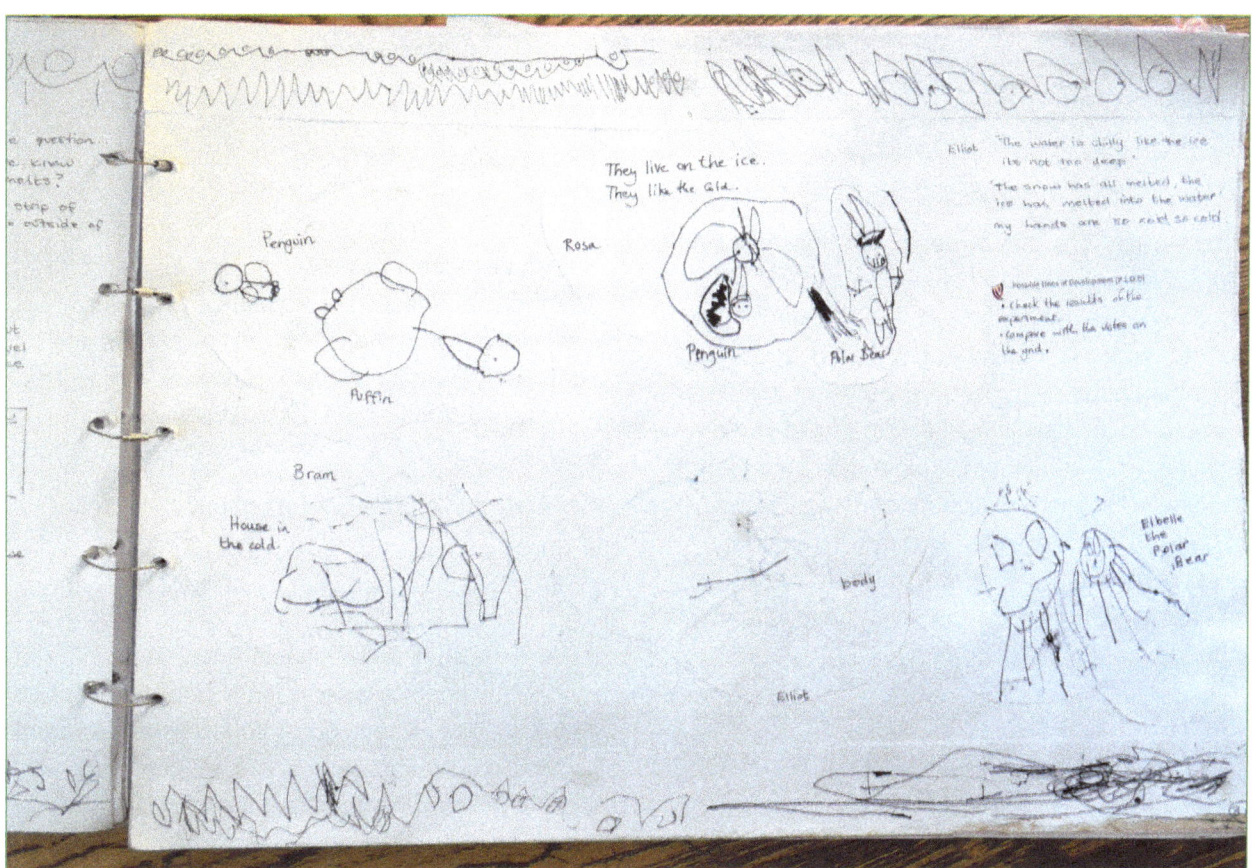

Stages of writing through the creation of borders

SECTION 1. PEDAGOGICAL THINKING BEHIND FLOORBOOKS

Every day we can use handwriting to:
- remember things
- organise ourselves
- reconstruct information
- reflect on experience
- communicate with others
- clarify ideas
- report on events
- share opinions
- entertain
- persuade.

Children rereading their own words

Writing in context

- communication about something that matters, such as letters, pamphlets, stories or messages
- a way of remembering minutes of meetings, or recording ideas or plans
- an enjoyable, thought-provoking process and one of beauty.

When asked why they write, a child may frequently reply, 'because the *teacher* said so' but, as educators, we can embrace real-life opportunities, so that writing in a Floorbook can be enjoyed and used with purpose. Children experiment with their realities, so, just as adults need to model writing by hand, we also need to explore the rich ways we can use writing in our environments. The reality of the loss of handwritten text is the loss of the art of writing itself, along with letter formation and spelling, rather than the construction that can indeed be done on a screen.

Writing can be:
- a way of working through lists, jotters, diagrams, drafts and doodles
- a means of reflection through journals, logs, notes and poems
- preparation for non-written opportunities, such as writing a script for a film or writing a shopping list for cooking

A Floorbook engages children in the process of writing because it has meaning and relevance to them. The abstraction of writing on to screens has removed many of the more traditional ways and purposes of writing by hand. However, the sense of audience remains the same. We write for:
- ourselves
- family and people we care about
- friends
- other people who *we want* to communicate with.

It is this sense of audience that is important in making the book accessible in the book corner or on a table when children come into a session. Children come to rely on it as a place for communication generally. When the adult lays the foundation and openly accepts the opportunity, children use it to send messages, save copies of rough plans and connect with each other when working on joint projects. In that sense it is a working document, a place for making the thinking process more visible between children and adults and across time.

SECTION 1. PEDAGOGICAL THINKING BEHIND FLOORBOOKS

Exploring line

Writing as a holder of memory

I believe it was Theodor Seuss Geisel who said that you don't know how important a moment is until it becomes a memory. So much of a child's learning process is about moments and they go by at an astounding rate. In day-to-day experiences, children see us make notes and throw them into the recycling but also observe us save a note from a friend and put it on the wall. Consider how the children in your environment see adults using writing and what that tells them about its worth.

Writing can be:

- thrown away when it has done its job
- sent back with a reply
- published for others to read
- kept and valued
- used as a basis for a discussion.

All these points relate to our perception of writing. Writing to learn or indeed learning to write is not only about letter formation or learning phonics. In a co-constructive environment for play and learning, writing can be:

- displayed in a draft and in a finished form to share the perseverance and effort involved in writing
- collected and shared in anthologies, story-books or magazines
- used for planning next steps that are meaningful and connected
- taken home to share or develop ideas with family and friends
- put in libraries so that the knowledge and thinking can be shared over time and across age groups
- kept as a record of progress for the child and external agencies.

The relevance for me, in the contexts of digital documentation and hard copy, is related to the purpose. I support the ease of connection between electronic learning stories and the parents and family who surround the child, but for me, documentation is so much more than just communication of a moment that has occurred. When a Floorbook is co-created and placed into the hands of the child or children, it becomes an integral part of a learning strategy, not only for writing but for all domains of learning and indeed of the child's self-perception that they are a confident individual and a motivated learner. It is important to remember that Floorbooks are about writing and are therefore really effective at engaging children in the communication of writing and reading that embraces speaking and listening.

We develop our capability to communicate, and specifically to write, when we:

- have a chance to experiment with mark-making
- talk about the process of writing and can ask questions about it
- can share the process and write collaboratively with our friends
- can read back our own writing and that of our friends
- can look at our writing from over a long period and see how we have developed the look of our work
- feel we are in a place where people want to communicate with us
- experience value and respect for our language and way of communicating
- can write alongside an adult who models how to write.

These aspects and all those discussed above are contained within a Floorbook. We write alongside children with intent, and value what they say, make, do and write in such a way that the Floorbook itself operates as a hub for the learning journey of a group of children. The features and strategies in Sections 2 and 3 are designed to build on these foundations of communication. Floorbooks align with inquiry-based learning because they are open and responsive, adapting as the journey evolves. Through holding on to the features of a Floorbook, we centralise co-construction in our pedagogy and make the relationships and connections between our experiences and opportunities more visible, rather than just recalling them separately.

The following case study in an infant school started with a group of children in a school exploring a line but, in response to the children, the experience shifted and changed to become an inquiry into identity.

Exploring line

Case study: From a line to a family
by Jenny Hutchinson (UK)

Child B experimented by drawing precursive patterns and shapes using the pens provided within the 'writing area' of continuous provision. Initially, the child's mark-making skills appeared quite delicately placed, but after adult intervention, her grasp became much more confident and robust. Child B began re-creating her own precursive patterns using the whiteboard pens, paper and resources available. The practitioner quickly introduced a variety of different mark-making tools to the child and she began exploring line using different mediums.

The practitioner asked the child to describe the lines that she was drawing and creating. Language rapidly developed and the child explored new vocabulary, such as *thick, thin, curly, jagged, zig-zagged, swirly, dotted* and *wavy*, to describe her lines. The practitioner then introduced the work of famous artist Bridget Riley to the whole class. She asked the children to 'make marks' using thick and thin paintbrushes. The whole group then explored vocabulary relating to pattern, shape, space and line, all based on the artist's style. Their pieces were displayed in the class (top right photo).

Exploring line

Further incorporating child-initiated play

Child B then accessed the drawing area to model to her friends how to implement these new-found line drawing skills. Child B noticed that a peer had drawn a picture of himself and his family on to brown parcel paper in the creative area. Child B commented, 'You have drawn curvy and wavy lines there.'

After catching the attention of the practitioner, Child B repeated her remark. The practitioner then explored lines used within the child-initiated family portrait, focusing on facial features. The children explored, in detail, the different lines and shapes that lie within the human aspect. These simple line-drawn family and self-portraits were then immediately displayed on the class 'learning journey' display board.

Displays of learning pathways in accessible places in and outside the classroom

SECTION 1. PEDAGOGICAL THINKING BEHIND FLOORBOOKS

Documenting and displaying the children's interests

The children in the class were then asked to draw an individual self-portrait using the skills Child B had taught them. This collective gallery formed the entranceway or 'doorway to learning display' outside the classroom door. This documentation was used to welcome any visitors inside the classroom.

Further encouraging the children's interest in the inquiry

The children were engaged in the 'family' inquiry and explored creative skills, such as line drawing, that they could use to represent family and self-portraits. Soon a monochrome 'family' display using simple child-drawn pictures was created to celebrate their learning.

Exploring people through lines (above and left)

Keeping the children engaged over a prolonged period and the evolving inquiry

All children remained highly engaged and wanted to make more and more 'people' or family members. The practitioner developed their newly acquired artistic skills and extended the choice and dexterity by using natural collage materials. The children used the available resources found within the classroom environment to create their 'people'. These creations formed the basis of our 'Making learning visible' display board.

Making learning visible

SECTION 1. PEDAGOGICAL THINKING BEHIND FLOORBOOKS

The children regularly referred to this documentation when accessing the continuous provision. They used large-scale recycled materials positioned and readily available from the building area to create large models of themselves. Children even brought leaves inside the classroom after playtime to use in their 'people' collage creations.

What began with a line drawn by a child, metaphorically spiralled and steered the whole class into a child-initiated learning process, focused purely on the children's interests. This approach evolved naturally with the children, therefore immersing them fully within the line of inquiry of identity.

Extending learning through collage

SECTION 1. PEDAGOGICAL THINKING BEHIND FLOORBOOKS

The next section explores how to create a rich environment that supports all children to share their theories and experiences of the world around them in the Floorbooks so that they become reflective of the social justice we support.

Inclusive practice

All children have the right to be heard and to communicate. The concept of inclusivity is, for me, about adapting the methods you use so that diverse children can share what they know in a way that works for them. Such adaptations may be for a child who only attends one day a week or has English as a second language, but to be truly inclusive we need to be responsive, including in our planning process. This approach involves the following aspects, which help to convey the incredible value the Floorbooks have as a means of encouraging social justice.

Valuing diverse scripts and languages

- Accept children fully as they are at the moment you meet them rather than for their potential attainment in the future.

Sharing individual moments

- Adapt the way you work with a Floorbook. Always begin with the child's own knowledge, accommodate to help them share and acknowledge their contribution as valued and unique.

Individual pages within the group Floorbook

- With consistent inclusion, no one is left behind and everyone is part of the group. Separating a child signals they are different. However, whatever a child communicates goes into the same Floorbook; for example, sign language, multiple languages, eye movement and even body posture are all included, equal and visible.

- In positioning yourself as the adult, adopt a rights-based perspective that values everyone, rather than a deficit model. The implicit message you send is often non-verbal. Adapt your interaction during a session with the Talking Tub or Floorbook by making fine adjustments, such as *holding the space* for the child to think, to reframe language, to make eye contact or not.

- Provide clear and concise feedback for children in a Floorbook; focusing on the effort and the thinking, not on attainment or results.

Child-created games included in the main Floorbook

37

SECTION 1. PEDAGOGICAL THINKING BEHIND FLOORBOOKS

- When an adult rereads the Floorbook with an individual or a group, they can then give clear, positive and productive feedback: 'I saw the way you shared with John to make your den. I wonder what you will do next?'
- The contextual nature of Floorbooks responds to those children who need opportunities to connect to real-world learning, responds to their interests and allows them to share what they know through active experiences.
- Many children with special rights benefit from revisiting learning over long blocks of time. A day becomes a week, and a week turns into a month. Slowing down and revisiting your own thinking is referred to as metacognition and it is an integral part of Bruner's spiral of learning and Vygotskian thinking around the zone of proximal development.
- A collective of individuals can achieve social change. The values you hold and practise as a team are visible in the practice shared through the Floorbook. Our work in nature pedagogy has been supported by the years of work collated and made accessible to a variety of audiences through Floorbooks.

Floorbooks are flexible to respond to the needs of any group – children, parents or the staff team. This flexibility exists because you can:

- adapt the pace and content in inquiry-based play to suit the needs of children
- appeal to children who struggle to grasp concepts through seat-based activities by using real-world learning and the Talking Tubs
- offer opportunities for children inside, outside and beyond the gate and value them all equally

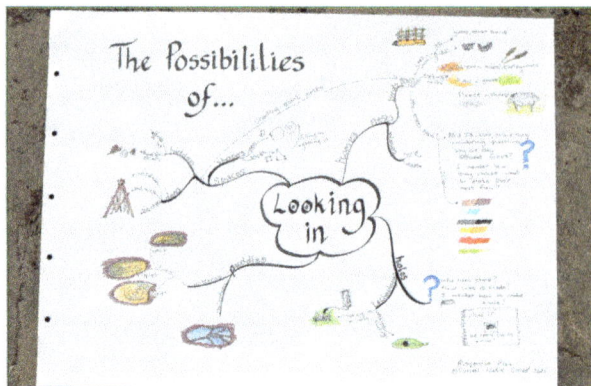

Visual mind map

- use a Talking Tub to engage children and listen to and observe their thoughts
- include all contributions and value visual, auditory and kinaesthetic learners equally
- enable children to contribute to the Floorbook at a range of times and in a variety of ways that respond to their confidence to communicate.

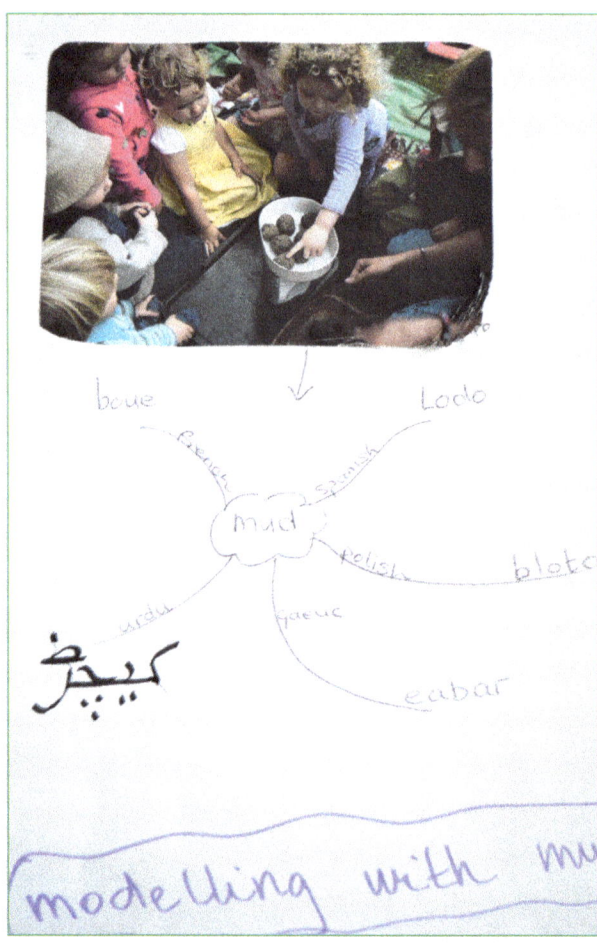

Using Floorbooks outside

As the study discussed below suggests, practice that fosters creativity can be seen as being 'learner inclusive', in taking children's ideas seriously. Learner-inclusive practices involve children and teachers co-participating in the learning context.

Such close interplay between children and adults in relation to fostering creativity has been documented closely in research in a small number of classrooms in England with children aged three to seven years (Burnard et al 2006; Cremin et al 2006). The study involved working closely with staff in three separate settings to investigate both their pedagogic practices and the children's learning. The research team identified several distinct but interlinked core features of learners' and teachers' engagement that each setting valued and fostered.

- **Asking questions.** Educators with a concerned, deep knowledge of each individual child closely documented their questions, including both those asked aloud and others implied through actions. They treated the questions with respect and interest, and nurtured and celebrated them. Question-posing often occurred in imaginative play.

- **Play.** Children in these settings were offered opportunities to play over extended periods. They were highly motivated and engaged, deeply interested and very serious in their playfulness, engaging closely with one another's ideas and experience, imagining all kinds of scenes, encountering and solving problems.

- **Immersion.** In each setting, children were deeply immersed in a caring, positive, loving environment, which was combined with overt cognitive challenge.

- **Innovation.** Children made strong and playful connections between ideas in their own ways. Educators encouraged them to do this and sought to further the children's growing understandings, offering provocations to stimulate connection-making.

Talking and Thinking Tree as an active space for sharing ideas

- **Being imaginative.** Through imagining and being imaginative, children were able to be decision-makers about the quality of ideas, content of their learning tasks and ways of conducting them.

- **Self-determination and risk-taking.** Children were enabled in taking risks, working in safe, secure and supportive environments that expected them to exercise independence (agency) in making decisions and valued their contributions. Adults encouraged learning from experience as both empowering and generative. They worked hard not to rush children.

Creating an environment for nature pedagogy (top). Floorbooks include writing during play (bottom)

The study highlighted the significance of the enabling context in supporting playfulness in teachers and children, and encouraging self-confidence and self-esteem. Adults intentionally valued children's 'agency' – that is, children's abilities to have ideas and see these through interactions. They assumed and encouraged children's motivation, which other studies show is vital to high engagement as an indicator of high-quality learning in early childhood education (Laevers 1993; Pascal and Bertram 1997). The educators in the 2006 study offered children time and space to have ideas and see them through. They stepped back, so children's activity led their support of learning. Stepping back and empowering children for increasing blocks of time does not mean adult intent was absent. The reverse is true, in that educators needed to think very deeply before they made the decision.

SECTION 1. PEDAGOGICAL THINKING BEHIND FLOORBOOKS

Thinking about practice

Purpose

Before using Floorbooks, it is important to consider their purpose so that you can ensure they support intentional teaching, are relevant to children and are of high quality. Use the questions below to frame their purpose in your setting and be clear about how to make the whole approach sustainable.

- How will you encourage all children to contribute? If using the books for planning as well as documenting, how will you show the link?
- How will you maintain consistency?
- Who will manage the process?
- How will the books become an integral part of your planning process?
- Will the Floorbooks form part of an existing system for planning for learning? If so, how will they evidence planning?
- Will you use the Floorbooks to monitor coverage of experiences and outcomes in a more formal curriculum? If so, how?
- Will you use the Floorbooks as evidence of skills, knowledge and concepts across learning areas? If so, which areas show through most effectively? How will you draw attention to this?

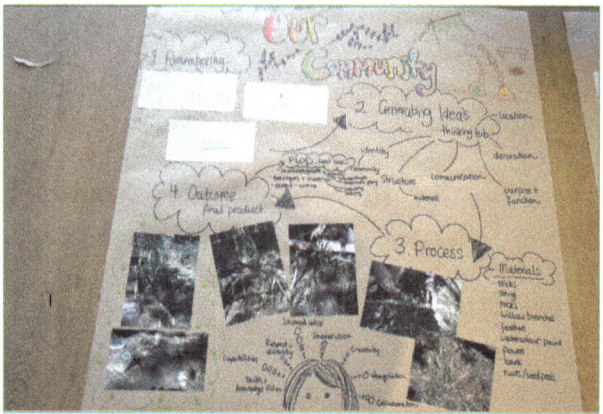

Understanding of practice

Form of Floorbook

The Floorbook is in essence a hub of many types of observation and documentation. It supports a social pedagogy that has identified strategies that work effectively to support children to share what they think. Ask yourself:

- What format works for you, your team and the children in your setting?
- Where will you store and display Floorbooks?
- If you are a nature preschool or kindergarten or a forest school and spend the majority of time outdoors, how will you use and share the Floorbooks? What size is manageable if you are moving about a lot?
- When you have continuous provision that uses both the inside and the outside, where will you position the Floorbook to celebrate learning in each location? Are there ways that you can lift moments from the Floorbook to make learning visible outside?

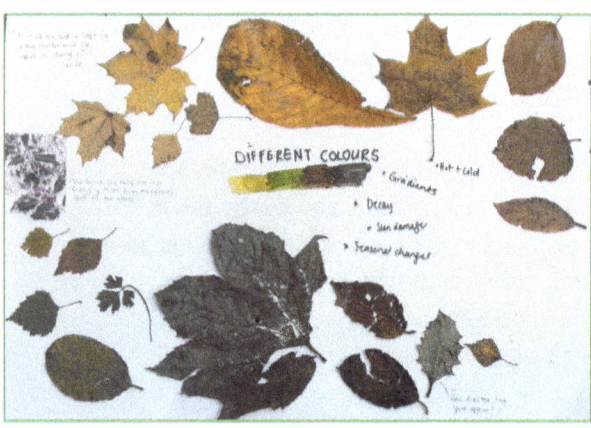

Adults experiencing the process (top) and thinking about the process (bottom)

SECTION 1. PEDAGOGICAL THINKING BEHIND FLOORBOOKS

Management

As with any recording process, many people contribute to Floorbooks. To make the use of Floorbooks sustainable and maintain their high quality, it is useful to ask yourself:

- Who will contribute to the Floorbooks (eg, educators, parents, children, siblings, community visitors, visiting specialists)?
- Who is responsible for managing the process (eg, lead educator or key group leader)?

Discussion as a staff team

We all know how rapidly time seems to pass by. If the Floorbook is to value and respect children's ideas and theories, it is worth spending a few moments looking at, thinking about and discussing how the team feel the Floorbook will develop.

- When will you use the Floorbook – on an ongoing basis or for a defined block of time?
- Over what block of time will the Floorbook develop? All year? Two weeks? Termly?
- Who will use the Floorbook and how often? For example, will any child who wishes to for one hour every day, or will each key group of children use it with their educator?
- In infant–toddler rooms, how often will the adults create a page? Where will you keep it – for example, on the floor in a large plastic pocket or low down on a wall behind a plastic sheet?

Training

To understand the Floorbooks, we need to understand the development of language and its wide role in the acquisition of knowledge, skills and attitudes. The place of oracy and the desire to communicate motivate children and adults to share more as long as the relationship between practice and paperwork remains effective and sustainable.

Giving ourselves time for training can move us from completing a Floorbook as a collection of moments to identifying and guiding the learning journey that is held within it to support all children to flourish.

To think about the place of educator research and review alongside published research, ask yourself:

- How will you share the process of consulting children across the setting?
- How will all staff be trained to understand the philosophy of creating a Floorbook?
- What strategies are in place to support staff to provide a provocation or question?
- How can you use Floorbooks to share the development of thinking and practice in the setting?

Having explored the thinking behind the Floorbooks and how to prepare to use them, let us move to the features within the books themselves.

Training in the Floorbook Approach

41

Section 2.
Features

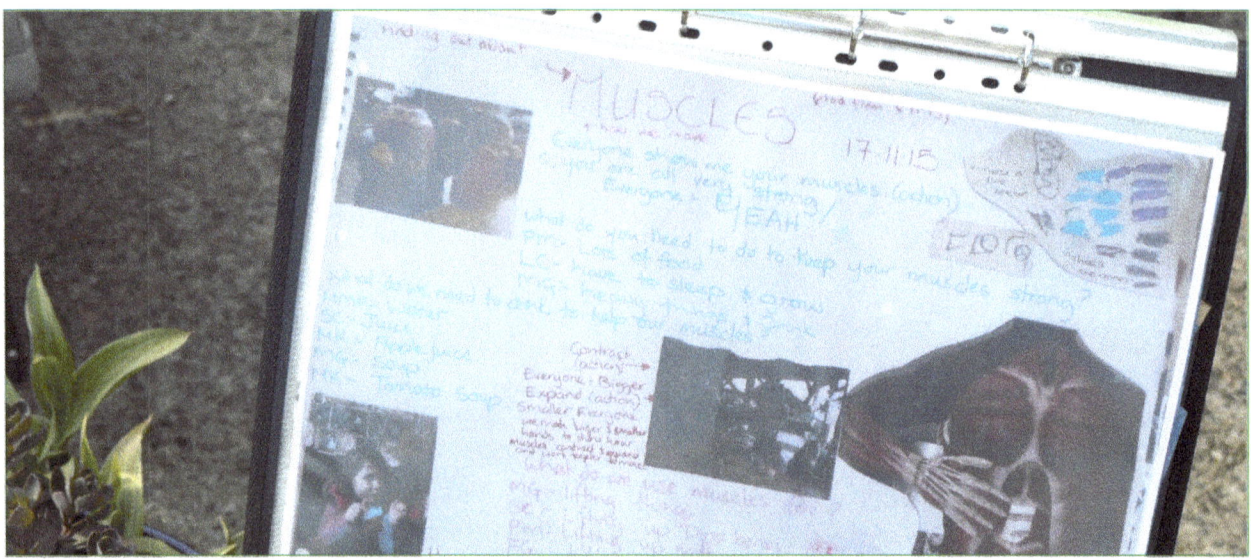

Certain key features make a Floorbook identifiable. These features are of course place-based and responsive, which means that the way in which each one is represented is unique to each Floorbook. Nobody can undertake the same open-ended inquiry in exactly the same way as someone else – that is the joy of the approach. Through considering and being mindful of these features, we can embrace philosophy, empowerment, agency, progression and accountability, as this section outlines.

We begin by considering the philosophy of the adults using Floorbooks and how this aligns with the pedagogical principles in the setting and the purpose of using the whole Floorbook Approach.

♥ Philosophy

Positioning a series of questions in Section 1 was intentional as a way of prompting you to define the current philosophy and pedagogy both within yourself and within the wider context of the setting in which you work. Understanding your own standpoint – or your *world view* as the research refers to it – is important because it affects everything you do, from your decisions about how to present a learning opportunity, to your focus on children's rights. Your world view has emerged through your lived experiences, your training and professional life, encompassing everything down to the books you have chosen to read.

If we explore the image of the child and move away from single theorists such as Malaguzzi, Froebel or Montessori, we can explore the constructs of children (Sorin and Galloway 2006) through comparing the image of the child, the image of the adult and the balance of power in the relationship. As noted in the Introduction, relationships with each other and those around you are central to a socially based pedagogy.

Oracy embedded in the environment

Table 2.1 explores just a selection of images of the child as well as what each one means in terms of the adult role and the balance of power.

SECTION 2. FEATURES

Table 2.1: Comparing the images of the child and adult and their implications for the balance of power

Image of the child	Image of the adult	Power of the child	Power of the adult
The child is innocent, carefree and uncomplicated, a blank slate.	**The adult is protector and leader** who makes decisions for the children.	Child has little power.	Adult has a lot of power.
The snowballing child seems to be in charge of the people around them.	**The deferring adult** does not set limits and so cannot negotiate.	Child gains power and it snowballs.	Adult could have power, but hands it over to the child.
The child is **a miniature adult**, essentially the same as an adult.	**The adult is mature.**	Power lies in the child's ability to learn in a world that the adult creates.	Power is seen in knowledge and can be used to guide or control.
The agentic child is capable and confident. In this optimistic view, the child is an active, social actor.	**The adult is a co-constructor** of being that benefits both adult and child.	Power is negotiated.	The adult shares their power through consultation and dialogue rather than imposing ideas.

Source: Adapted from Sorin and Galloway (2006, p 21)

What do these images mean for the use of Floorbooks and Talking Tubs? If we view the table as reflecting a hierarchy of power, then we can see that an adult who feels protective of children will plan, design and create the Floorbook by themselves, taking away the need for children to be involved, apart from in the play.

Children's agency

Accessibility of the Floorbook

SECTION 2. FEATURES

Children's many ways of knowing

In contrast, the adult who believes in empowering children sees negotiation and consultation as part of their rights, not as a requirement. In this more balanced approach, Floorbooks that share adult-intent and child-created content will show evidence of collective decision-making such as voting, meetings and plans.

The starting point

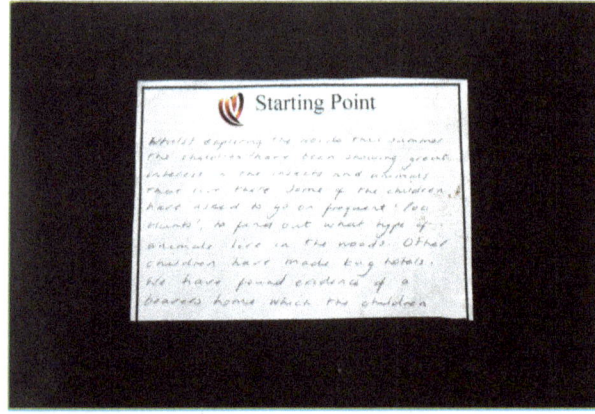

Starting point

There are many reasons for starting a learning journey in a Floorbook. It is usually in response to an opportunity that has emerged from an adult's thinking or the children's, or preferably both.

When an adult creates an invitation to engage in an inquiry, it is in response to a need to explore a curriculum or learning area, such as risk management, that they believe has not been addressed.

Children who have not been surrounded by rich, engaging opportunities from birth may not initially offer ideas in planning for the inquiry. In these environments, the adult creates the Talking Tub in response to what they feel children are interested in and then uses that as the platform to leap off into an inquiry. We will look at the place of Talking Tubs and how to create them in Section 4.

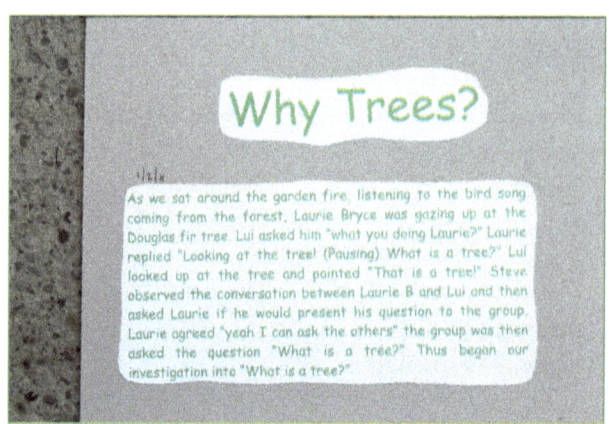

Sharing why an inquiry begins

Where children feel more agentic and are aware of the possibilities in front of them, ideas and plans can emerge and be recorded easily in a Floorbook.

To position the inquiry, place a note on the inside front cover detailing the circumstances that led to the start of the learning journey held within the Floorbook. By looking back over several Floorbooks, the team can monitor the balance of child-led and adult-led provision.

Authorship and agency

Sign-in sheet

The desire to write stems from many facets. One of them is feeling valued and respected as a writer, which is the reason behind the ritual of asking children to sign in on the first page before the learning journey starts. If children or any visiting adults join you through the inquiry, they are invited to go back to the sign-in page and add a note or picture that shows they are now part of the learning journey.

The second page in the Floorbook often has questions, ideas and comments about the inquiry that can be extended over time.

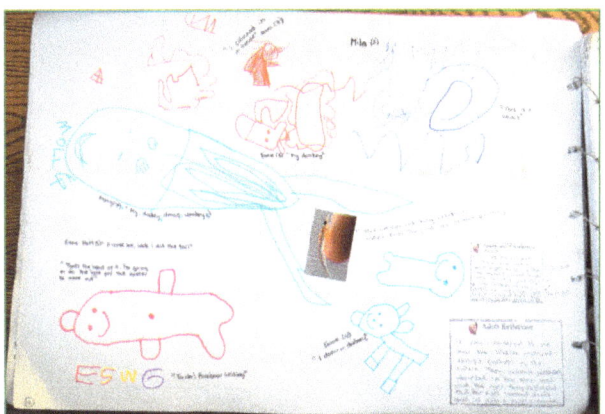

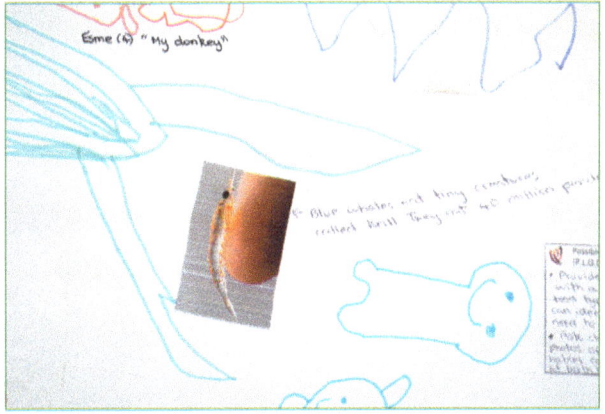

Children's fascination with whale food

During these initial group sessions, we talk about:

- what we already know – children come to any moment with life experiences. Through noticing, listening, valuing and documenting this embedded knowledge, we can tune in to their knowledge and avoid unnecessary duplication
- any questions that come to us – questioning is a higher-order thinking skill that may not emerge as formed questions until five or six years old. Younger children, however, are curious, and the adult may notice a facial gesture and a statement where the question comes through in the intonation of the voice, such as 'Dog has legs?'. We use the phrase 'I wonder' in these sessions so that children hear the open-ended nature of inquiry
- our motivation and enthusiasm – inquiries should build on curiosity and a sense of adventure, both physically and metaphorically. Without these elements, learning can be very dull. The real-world learning at the foundation of this work gives children a link to step from the known into the unknown. Although we all have varying levels of enthusiasm for our work, these playful inquiries should be motivating

Front cover of Floorbook

- our ideas and plans for the inquiry – agency is related to a sense of empowerment, as noted in Table 2.1 (page 43). Consulting children is more than documentation, as we established in Section 1. A Floorbook demonstrates that philosophy in practice every time we use it.

Children share their thinking on the tree

During or shortly after this process, the adult is stepping back mentally to observe the broader picture and to consider the engagement and

SECTION 2. FEATURES

response of the group or individual as part of a formative assessment process. This process allows the adult to adjust what they do or provide for the individual or group to meet their needs.

Gathering for a Talkaround Time

When we gather together, we have the ritual of putting out the round, black mat and singing a gathering song: 'Everybody, everybody, come this way; everybody, everybody, Talkaround Time.' This ritual is only used for the group time for these sessions. Taking an image at the start of the inquiry where the group is talking generally gives evidence of the process of consultation and that there is a focus on conversation, as an open exchange, and dialogue, which has a more defined purpose.

Floorbooks support adults to have ownership and agency

Many features throughout a Floorbook demonstrate their authorship and agency. For example, children cut out and stick down the images, decorate the page borders and are writers on the pages. Floorbooks also include little books the children make, and link to mark-making done at any point during the day, whether at home or in the setting.

The bringing together of an inquiry moves the Floorbook into its final stages. It is the point where the front cover is finished, and the pages are revisited to complete or indeed reflect on the experiences documented.

Little books created by children

Traces of play-based writing

Tracking flow and progression

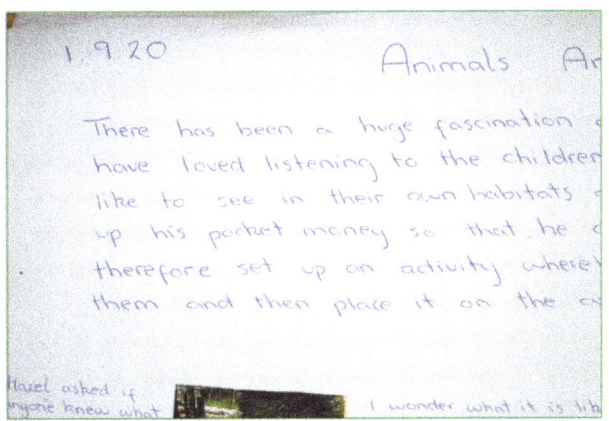

Floorbook entries with page numbers and dates

Tracking children's learning allows us to monitor the progression in their thinking. As engaged adults, we can sense when learning is moving forward through recalled facts or the application of concepts but in some cases, we want to monitor our practice, the group and individuals in more detail.

Practice

One of the common criticisms of open-ended inquiry is that it does not have the rigour that traditional formal education has. The reality is that although evidence can be gathered from worksheets, some of them provide evidence only of an ability to complete a form, rather than an ability to apply the concept, use the skill or build on the knowledge. Playful inquiries that are co-constructed, as opposed to being fully child-led, provide opportunities to learn core skills and explore concepts and pieces of knowledge *and* provide children with long blocks of time to apply the new content.

The term *schema* describes both the mental and physical actions involved in understanding and knowing. Schemas are categories of knowledge that help us to interpret and understand the world. Floorbooks are full of them as they note what children think and do. In Piaget's view, a schema includes both a category of knowledge and the process of obtaining that knowledge. As experiences happen, this new information is used to modify, add to or change previously existing schemas.

Piaget referred to the stage of exploring a new idea as *application*, the process of thinking differently because of new experience as *accommodation* and the final stage of internalising new learning as *assimilation* (Scott 2019). Piaget also referred to *equilibration*, which is where children seek a balance between accommodation and assimilation. We can track the non-linear process of learning through creating a dated record. We can then use this in the learning journey mind map at the back of the Floorbook to guide a new reader through the loops and changes of direction that learning follows in a playful inquiry.

Group

Every child is included in the Floorbook. In large early years environments, it is the role of the key person to ensure that their group has rich, engaging opportunities around them that are co-constructed but also free from adult intent.

Group map-making to show a sense of place

A Floorbook is an effective tool in adult dialogue for exploring consistency and quality across a team. The images taken, the words noted and the flow of the book give wonderful evidence to support educator reflection by themselves, with a mentor or with a group of colleagues.

Individual

It is important to celebrate every child in the book as an individual, as well as part of a learning community. In a busy setting, their inclusion will need to be tracked, especially for children who attend part time, have complex rights or use multiple languages.

SECTION 2. FEATURES

As noted in the Introduction, a large Floorbook is one of four key strategies that are used to share the learning. Another is a Family Book, which is full of individual learning stories (Carr and Lee 2012) that emerge from either the Floorbook or the wider play opportunities. Using images and stories in two locations is more time effective, creating more time for playful interactions.

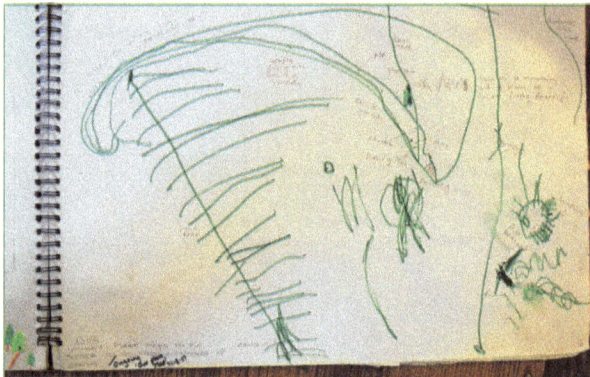

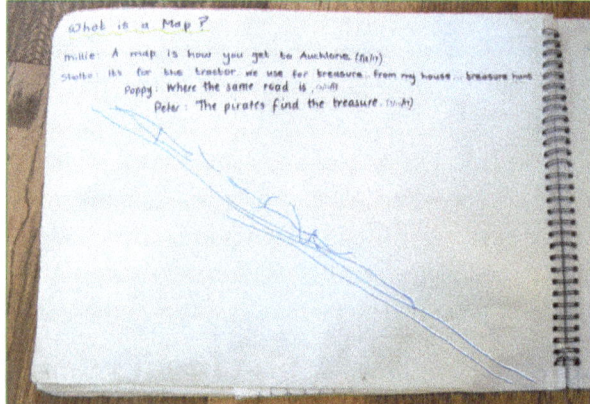

Individual responses to the group inquiry on mapping

When older children use the Floorbooks, the direct teaching of core skills often happens first. Later the evidence of the application of the concept, skill or knowledge is gathered from the Floorbook and put into Learning Journals.

👁 Noticing

Our ability to not only be with children but really notice them – what they say, feel and do – is pivotal to a journey of inquiry. As a child drags a stick along the ground, are we aware of what they are exploring? In nature-based pedagogy, we need to look beyond the material, the moment and the resource to see, to really notice what is being explored, applied and learnt. Using simple materials can provide complex learning; however, the reality is that the real benefit comes when children use what appear to be simple materials such as a leaf, a stick or a block and have an adult alongside them who can see it. In these moments, conversations and dialogue can take place that deepen thinking, but at the same time the educators are adopting a dual role as they also think about practice. When they notice children, they are:

- aware of inclusivity

- aware of *all* children

SECTION 2. FEATURES

- considering the social connections to each other

- thinking about where children choose to be

- considering how children engage with invitations

- noticing engagement in an experience

- considering children's focus

- listening to children's theories and ideas.

SECTION 2. FEATURES

Any experience is full of this duality. When we can use a Floorbook with and for children, it can assist us in our documentation and planning, making the process so much easier.

Digital documentation

Floorbooks are physical books, but they also function as a symbol for community-driven learning through playful inquiries. Using digital technology in a Floorbook Approach can increase a child's agency and voice, allowing them to become constructors of knowledge in the matters that are important to them (Fleet et al 2017). The use of an audiovisual camera opens up the sharing of the process of discovery; the macro lens allows us to see, select and document aspects of the natural world that would otherwise only be available on a television inside and controlled by someone else. Our very concept of knowledge has expanded to go beyond something in the minds of a few, to something that is globally accessible.

When using technology in documentation, however, it is important to consider questions such as:

- Why are you documenting?
- How will it make a difference to the child?
- Who is the audience?
- How will children revisit the documentation?
- To what extent do children feel any ownership of documentation if it is purely on screen?
- How does your documentation really link directly into your planning?

We explore some of these questions in detail in the following section on representation.

Kashmira Gander's (2019) project assessed whether the use of paper books or ebooks made any difference to the interactions between parents and children. She reported that:

> Parents and toddlers who read paper books together speak and interact more when compared with those who read e-books …

> Researchers found parents and toddlers spoke more when interacting with a paper book rather than a story on an electronic tablet. What's more, parents used richer language when using print books compared with tablets, and collaborated more with their children.

In planning with and for children, technology can help us and save us time but our reason for using it needs to be to enhance practice, not to drive it. The following images show how digital technology can enhance documentation but hold on to children's need to be physically involved in a Floorbook.

QR codes in a Floorbook (top and bottom)

Digital documentation used in a Floorbook (above and page 50)

SECTION 2. FEATURES

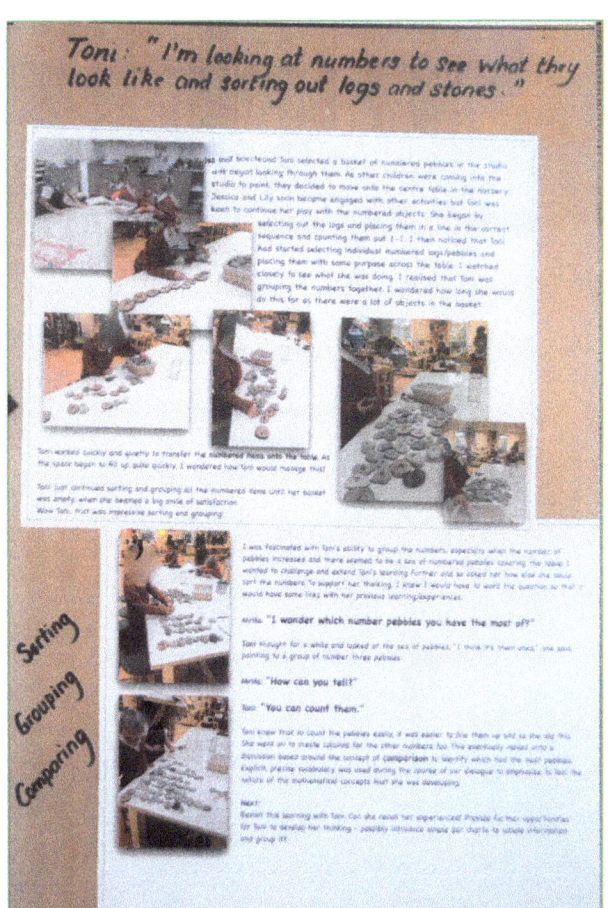

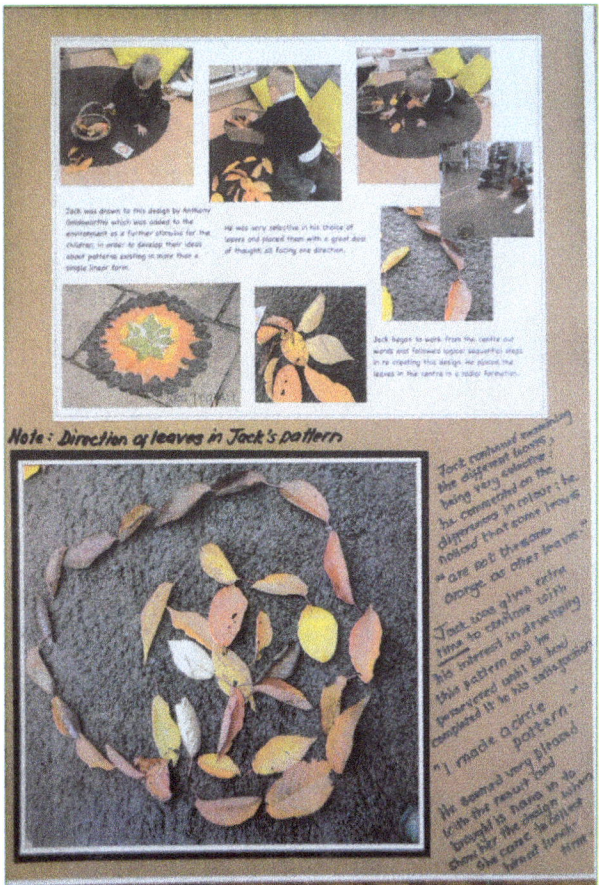

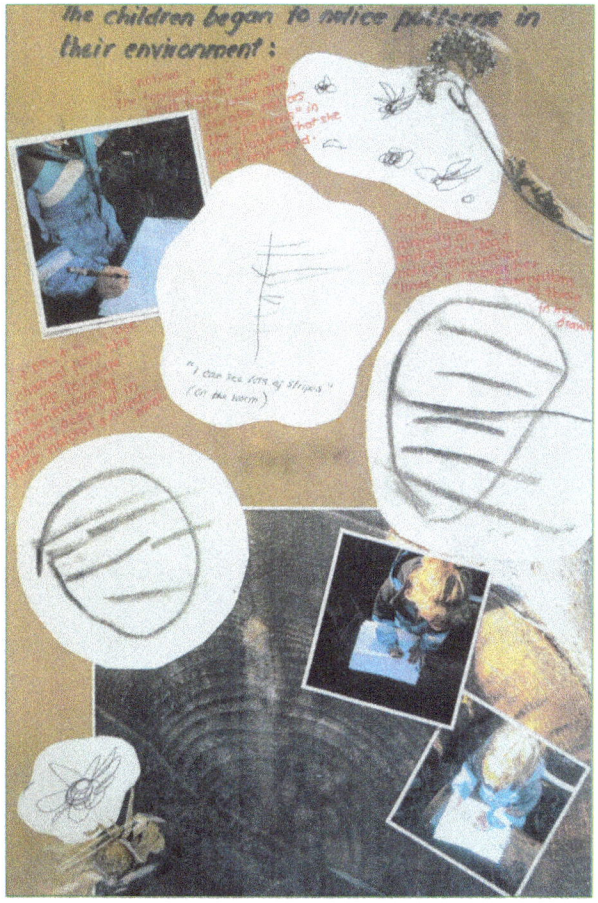

SECTION 2. FEATURES

It is not technology alone that supports the pedagogy. As Blackwell et al (2014) point out, the educator's knowledge, understanding and interpretations of child development allow for effective assessment for learning. Children's rights are central to this approach and the use of digital technologies needs to focus on active participation in their use so that, as Eaude (2011) suggests, it becomes a tool that children can use to steer their own learning.

The use of QR codes has brought physical Floorbooks and the digital world closer together. The QR code is essentially a hyperlink to a specific location on a secure site where snippets of film and audio are stored. If you print out the QR code and place it in the book at the location where children have been sticking in photos, writing or drawing, you can then use the QR scanner to enable the child or adult to watch the film or listen to the conversation all at the same time. This use of digital technology allows even greater depth, accuracy and authenticity to emerge from the pages of the Floorbook.

Representation

Children select the images they like

One of the benefits of technology has been to allow us to capture information easily. The insidious converse to this is that it has created the fear of missing a moment (jovially called *the beast of FOMAM* by our team).

Children need to be represented in a Floorbook in many ways. Many people have found inspiration in the work of Loris Malaguzzi around a Hundred Languages of Children in Reggio Emelia, which explores ways children can share what they know through talking, writing, modelling, making, singing and other activities, as we look at in Section 4. It is useful to monitor what experiences and opportunities children have so that children in settings have access to a broad, balanced provision. Some of the ways of knowing and sharing will be recorded through image and film rather than the item itself and in those moments, it is effective practice to share process rather than just the final product.

Recording what young children say is becoming easier with digital technology, but there is still a place for representing what the child says in written rather than printed text. When you are writing down what children say, your adult brain will select phrases and process them very quickly.

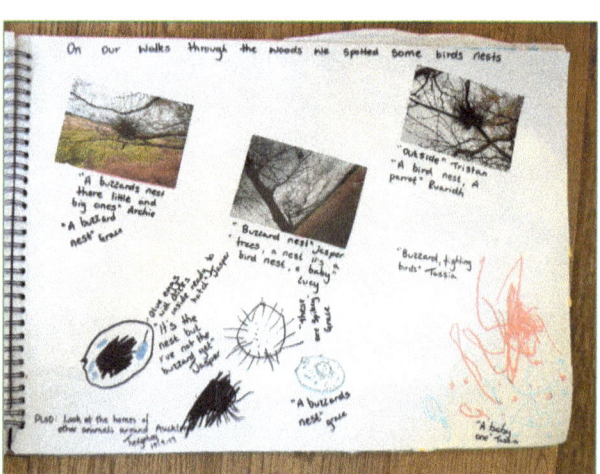

Children take the photos

It is important to note that you are aiming not to write everything down but to capture a few words or sentences that show what children are exploring in their thinking. For children who do not communicate through speech, we share their behaviour through a short descriptive passage.

Case study: Soup from the garden
by Nurture through Nature (Australia)

A few children had been making fairy gardens and the conversation had moved to thinking about what we wanted to explore together.

Creating a link to children's ideas through conversation

As the conversation then moved to making soup, it offered a real opportunity to explore vegetables in more depth, before deciding what we wanted to plant in the garden.

Making soup leads to learning about vegetables to plant

Our environment is set up to offer fiction and non-fiction books and we view the children's Floorbooks as an important part of our literacy experiences. Although making soup was the context, the skills explored were extensive.

Using Floorbooks for research and sharing (top) and for drawing ideas and plans (bottom)

SECTION 2. FEATURES

The garden and atelier area offered a range of media and opportunities to explore making soup. The images of making pretend soup and real soup were valued equally and included in the Floorbook. The subtle feeling of being and becoming came through easily as children used the Floorbook to look back on their experiences.

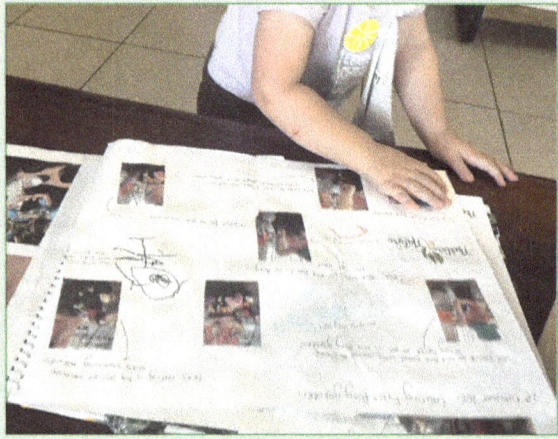

Looking back through the Floorbook (left) and finding herself represented on the page (right)

Consider these questions as you and the children select elements to put into the Floorbook.

- **Child rights.** How did you seek children's permission to be photographed or filmed? To what extent were children involved in choosing the elements to put in the Floorbook?
- **Authenticity.** How effective was the adult at writing down what the child said? Are the elements in the Floorbook truly representative of what the child did?
- **Purpose.** Is the purpose for including the image clear or does it need some explanation around it? Do the images selected tell the story? Do they show the process of play and inquiry?
- **Audience.** Who are the images and film for? Do too many show similar moments? Is everyone in the setting represented in the Floorbook in photos or another way?
- **Effectiveness.** Are the images selected a good use of time and worth the cost of printing? Do the pages reflect care and attention to detail? Are some pages child-led and others adult-led?

Creating a diagram to communicate an idea

Children and adults collaborate to complete a Floorbook. It is a working document rather than something that displays achievement so they complete some pages together whereas on others the adult takes the lead. I normally include pages that are created by children alone without adult involvement and they are often noted as such or described in a gently descriptive way in the corner to help the reader understand the agency children had to complete the page.

Contributions from the Thinking Tree and mind map sessions

The ritual of and routine access to the Floorbook allow children to understand the skill and process of sharing what they know. Floorbooks are often laid out on the table in the morning as children come in, with the printed images, scissors, paper cutter and glue available to them. In these moments the adult can invite children or let them choose to engage to stick in their image. This type of talk around recall and memory is different to talking about what is happening in the present and shows the development of connection and higher-order thinking. In some cases, the memory of the moment displayed in an image has gone and so the adult can come in as the holder of memories and share the story around the moment.

Children cut out and arrange their images

Community of the child, parents and educator

Families and educators sharing moments

There are three main voices in a Floorbook. The most visible is the child's voice, shared through image and word. Second, the parent or carer creates a bridge from home to the setting, making sense and links for the child to their wider social group and experience. Third, the educator notices, considers and analyses what ideas, plans and theories children have that they can take forward into creating a rich learning environment to extend their thinking.

SECTION 2. FEATURES

The Floorbook can also have a sprinkling of other voices. These voices come from the visitors and support specialists who can add a new perspective to the learning journey, including in relation to:

- home language
- cultural connections
- forms of communication, such as Braille
- a sense of place.

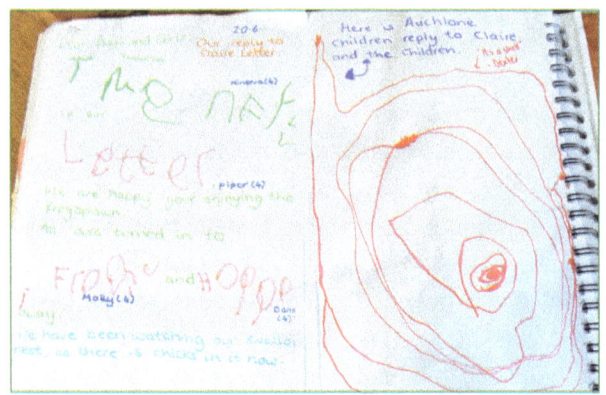

Positioning Floorbooks for children and families to share (top). Child contributions (middle). A letter to share with friends far away (bottom)

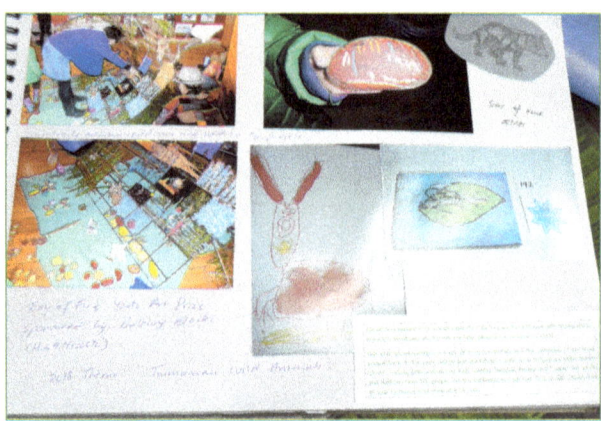

Including community events

If you adhere to a pedagogy that is about social constructivism, then that will also affect your engagement with parents, carers and the wider community. Although as individuals they may not complete a planning diary, the conversations and perceptions that the community around the child can offer make the content of the planning diary far more relevant for the children.

Child-created displays

As we noted in the Introduction, one of the four elements in the Floorbook Approach is the Communication Book, which collates cards, messages, thoughts and offers from the wider community (if you feel that the community should not have access to children's images). Taking an image of this book and putting it into the larger Floorbook helps children see and feel the value placed on their friends, grandparents and the wider community where they live. Consulting people gives value to their ideas and creates a more balanced relationship of power.

Case study: KIN Nature Kindergarten

by Sal Preston (UK)

KIN Nature Kindergarten is a completely outdoor early years setting for children aged two to five years. Located in Monmouthshire, it is the first of its kind anywhere in South Wales. Children attending the kindergarten spend up to five hours a day outside, all year round – whatever the weather.

At KIN we are passionate about giving children an unhurried childhood in nature. We value time and space in nature which allows children opportunities to connect with themselves, each other and the world around them.

We take a child-initiated approach to learning, preferring to use the children's interests, questions and theories as the starting point for our inquiries rather than planning activities based on a curriculum.

In contrast to traditional, practitioner-generated planning, the Floorbook is a highly visible and integral element of our kindergarten day. We produce this collaborative document with the children, and they have ownership of it and direct access to it. When the children arrive in the morning, the book is available for them to look through and add any photographs or extra thoughts or drawings from the previous day. We use it both as a reflective tool, to help children remember their previous learning and interests, and as a prompt for what they might like to do that day.

The child's voice lies at the heart of the Floorbook. It is the dominant voice and is documented using the child's exact words. The practitioner's voice runs alongside the child's but is quieter, offering context and possibilities for developing lines of inquiry. The curriculum sits in the background as a reference for coverage of skills.

The example page documents a session initiated by one of our older children. He was keen for us to have a fire as he had recently learnt how to build and light one. Before we moved to the fire circle, we discussed what we know about fire and how we should behave around one.

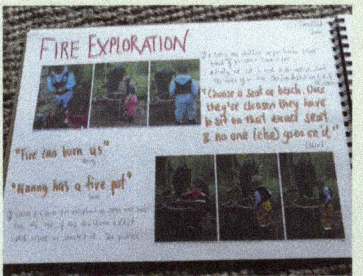

We have recently adopted the technique of audio- or video-recording our discussions with the children as it enables us as practitioners to be fully present in conversation with them rather than being distracted by taking notes. Elements of these discussions are transcribed into the Floorbook. The full discussion is then available by scanning the QR code. We have found that including the QR codes creates an additional opportunity for engagement with the Floorbook as children love to show it to their parents.

SECTION 2. FEATURES

Sharing the process of playful inquiries

Conversations about a Floorbook

Floorbooks make a real difference to team development, as the processes within playful inquiries are highly accessible. When a group of educators looks at Floorbooks together, the conversations are relevant and rich. The images, film and words all build a detailed picture to support their thinking.

The number of children who are linked to each book varies with their age and the setting. In some settings, a key worker has a group book for about 13 children, whereas in others 30 children may contribute to one book at different times.

Where a setting has a real focus on the development of practice, in terms of consistency the Floorbooks provide a window into what experiences children are having and how the staff are responding with intent.

Sharing the Floorbooks with other educators (bottom left). Exploring the positive effects of creative documentation (top right). Sharing the small steps though an experience (bottom right)

58

SECTION 2. FEATURES

In relation to participatory leadership, we use Floorbooks as a staff training and centre development tool. Educators start with initial ideas and thoughts, create action plans, research and responses and share both physical and pedagogical shifts in practice. These again include voices of all team members and the communities we work with. The same process and benefits apply to using Floorbooks with adults as they do with children. We create a real sense of agency, empowerment and motivation.

Adult focus on development areas (top). Continuing professional development materials in the Talking Tub (bottom)

Reflect – looking in, out, forward and back

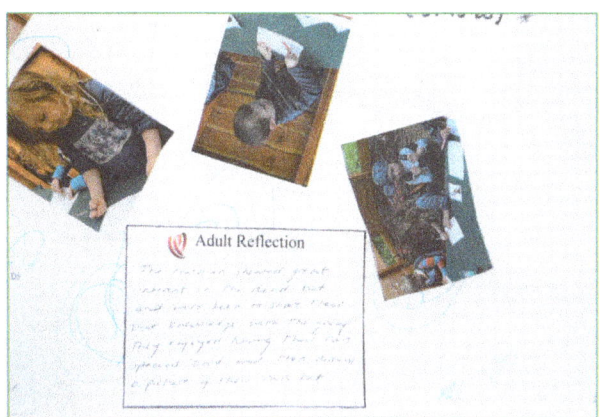

The process of thinking about what children say and do will occupy adults for millennia. It will never be perfect but the more that we listen and allow ourselves to step back to observe, the greater the chance that we will understand. Even then we need to allow space in our documentation and planning for children's agency to develop. With agency, power and leadership are negotiated so that children are consulted (Table 2.1, page 43).

Floorbook for adult-focused plans and reflections

When we come to reflect on the documentation in a Floorbook, we need to allow ourselves the same joyful indulgence to step into the memories that they contain. As adults we work very quickly, fully engaged in the day-to-day business with children, and looking at a Floorbook can give a real sense of affirmation to the staff team.

Looking in and out, back and then forward gives an indication of how your reflection needs to spread out into considering the journey you have been on as the adult, what influences are around you, what has happened, and where you and the children want to go to next.

Practically, we add a sticky rectangle on to a few pages that guide the educators to note down key points as the learning journey progresses rather than waiting until the end and trying to look back over an unhelpfully long period. Placing these rectangles in the same area on each of the pages increases the readability and accessibility of the book.

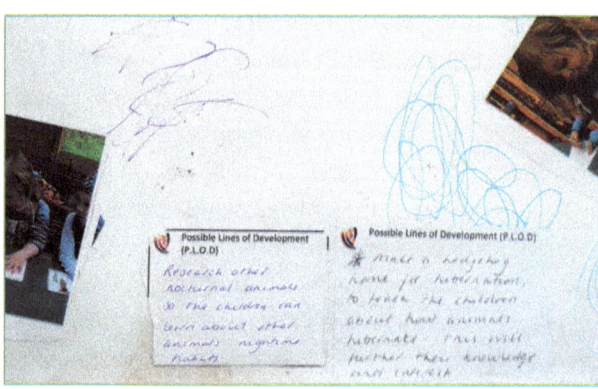

PLODs written in a Floorbook

Possible lines of development (PLODs)

If people just stuck pictures in a book, it would be a scrapbook – lovely but different from a Floorbook. Holding memories for children has a benefit, but when you combine these moments inside buildings, outside in play areas and beyond the gate into wilder spaces with an adult who is aware and intentional, the play and learning opportunities can expand exponentially. A possible line of development (PLOD) is written in a way that reflects its function to bring together a note of the experience or opportunity and its purpose. So we record what we plan to do and why we plan to do it. When looking at images of Floorbook pages, some people:

- make notes about them in a different colour so they stand out on the page
- place them in a defined space that is the same on each page so educators know where to look to find them
- fill in stick-on labels so that their intent is clear and all staff are encouraged to complete them.

Case study: Talking Tubs and Floorbooks
by Elizabeth McKie, Barrhill Early Years Centre (UK)

This local authority centre is part of Barrhill Primary School, South Ayrshire, Southwest Scotland. Children attend from 9 am to 3 pm, Monday to Friday, and we are fortunate to have a beautiful rural landscape and woodland areas on our doorstep. We strive to provide our children with high-quality learning experiences both indoors and in our wider community, taking full advantage of the natural beauty around us.

We complete formal planning documentation based on the needs and interests of the children, while taking into account the Curriculum for Excellence experiences and outcomes as well as local authority guidance. However, we felt that this style of documentation did not fully reflect the wonderful child-led experiences our children were engaged in and decided to use Floorbooks

Children exploring the Talking Tub

SECTION 2. FEATURES

alongside what was our planning format at the time. Since then, Floorbooks have become integral to our planning process. We are now able to document and highlight the full process from the first spark of the child's interest to the rich learning experiences that follow.

Recently, we observed that the children were becoming aware of the changing seasons and had been noticing leaves on the ground while we were walking in the local woods. They were particularly interested in the berries growing on the trees and bushes and in the acorns we found growing on an oak tree.

We introduced the children to our Talking Tub, which contained a variety of natural resources along with some photographs of woodland animals and autumn trees. We used it to begin to discuss and explore the many possible topics related to autumn.

Initially, the children were most interested in the seeds and acorns and the photos of squirrels. We explored all of these interests to see where these investigations would lead us. Children also had a general fascination with the weather and the changes in the trees. Further capturing their attention was how the river changed, as they noticed the water level was much higher and faster-flowing than it had been during the weeks before. One child surprised us with his own prior knowledge of rivers and water levels, and he was able to share this information with us through handling the materials. After documenting the design and creation of our own boats using natural materials, we added a photograph of this particular page of the Floorbook to this child's personal profile as this was a significant piece of learning for him.

Showing the process of play and discovery

SECTION 2. FEATURES

At the beginning of this journey, we thought that we would perhaps be exploring colour or pattern as lines of inquiry. Yet it turned out that the much wider concept of 'Changes' was the direction that the children led us in. We were impressed by their level of interest and engagement in decay and the varieties of mushrooms they were finding in the woodland area.

Possible line of development included in the Floorbook is linked to ongoing research

Children and adults write together in the Floorbook

We built on this engagement by doing some of our own research into the varieties of mushrooms that grow in the UK and comparing these to the ones we found. Our findings opened up conversations around risk management. The children shared their ideas, which we included in our Floorbook and risk assessment forms. A special moment came when one child found a mushroom growing up a tree next to the river and responded with huge excitement. It was lovely to share his enthusiasm when we looked back at the pages of the Floorbook months later.

The concept of being a possible line of development is just that – a possibility – and, for this reason, the number of PLODs on a page may be far greater than the number achieved. In the next section, we examine how you share the decision to follow one PLOD and not another.

✓ Demonstrating action and response

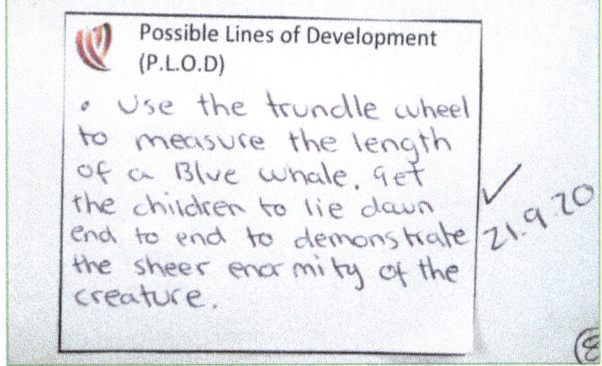

Action

After you have documented the process of play and children's ideas and thought through the PLODs, you should have many possibilities from a group of children. Deciding which one to start with is often the challenge. Consider the following points when you are deciding.

- **The broad interest of the wider group**, gathered from observations from the wider team. The Floorbook, as the hub, sits within the context of your setting. The experiences you plan will be part of a larger, continuous provision so making connections between rooms and across staff makes a more cohesive provision.
- **The drive and motivation** evident in the children, as documented in the Floorbook.

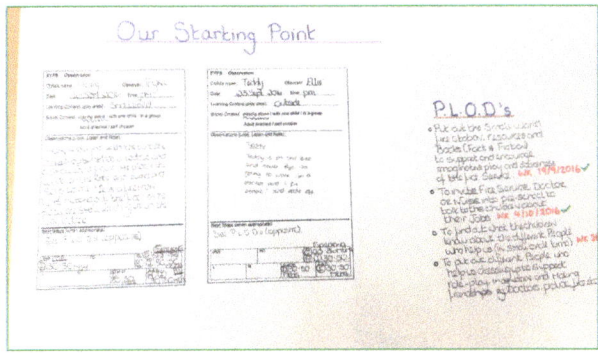

Noting starting point of the journey and the PLODs

Through listening to children, we come to know the style of inquiry they enjoy. For example, planning all seat-based activities for kinaesthetic children wouldn't be appropriate for them, so we consider the starting point and flow from there.

- **Potential for the PLOD to continue the learning journey** along the line of inquiry. Some experiences sit as isolated moments while others link together. Consider if the planned experience really connects to the central concept, skill, knowledge or indeed capacity.
- **Available resources.** Some specific resources may need to be gathered for the experience.
- **Access to space.** If the experience requires a lot of room, the environment may need to change to accommodate it.
- **Knowledge and skill of the adults** to engage in the experience. At times the opportunity that would extend children's thinking is just beyond the understanding of adults. As with Vygotskian thinking, we as adults can sit in the zone of proximal development, in which case we may need support from colleagues and to do further research.

The process of dating the PLOD when it has moved into a planning diary or on to a planning sheet has several benefits.

1. It provides evidence that listening to and consulting children has led to action; a change of some sort to meet their plans and needs.

2. It demonstrates that, from just one moment, play has the potential to spiral off along many tangents and that the team of adults in the setting has thought about these.

3. It shows that, rather than intending to always plan in the moment, the adult has the intent to develop patience and honesty as they acknowledge that they cannot organise the experience tomorrow but that it will happen next week. The key need is to be accountable to the children and to follow through. We can do that by going back to the page where the child's idea is recorded and then move forward.

SECTION 2. FEATURES

4. It allows us to share the leapfrogging in children's learning, the tapestry of how all the apparently separate parts link together in the mind of a child. A date where an experience took place then leads to a moment several pages later and that links to a moment a week after that. By dating and noting page numbers in the book, adults can follow a pathway and share that through the 2D mind map at the back of the book.

The learning journey – tracking learning inside, outside and beyond

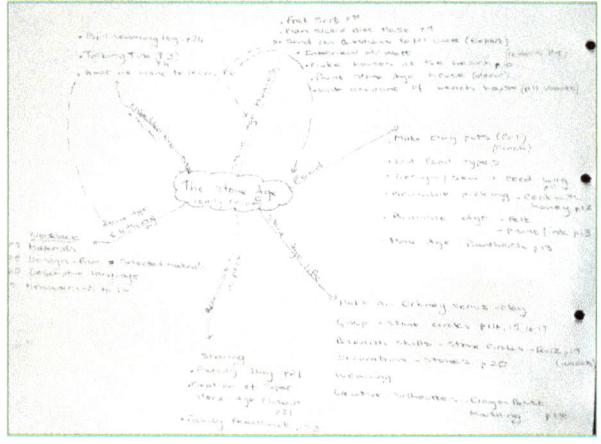

The learning journey – ancient peoples

We have established that learning is unpredictable and non-linear. One of the challenges in education is to balance the holistic nature and needs of children's learning with the needs and requirements for wider care and education. The learning pathway is not straight or simple, and yet we need to collect evidence and plan in a way that can link to a curriculum or a set of norms.

As the learning journey builds up in the Floorbook, the 2D mind map builds at the back of the book. Putting it and the curriculum at the back of the book keeps the adult reference material together.

On a particular page, the central title can be completed towards the end of the inquiry, but the lines of inquiry radiating out from it can be completed as the inquiry unfolds. By noting the PLODs along with the relevant date and page numbers at the end of the relevant line of inquiry, it is possible to gather a strategic overview of where the inquiry has been and where it is moving to. This allows you as the adult to decide to go with the flow or to revisit the Talking Tub and create an adult invitation because you feel that there are areas of learning that the children are not experiencing.

Accountability for breadth and balance

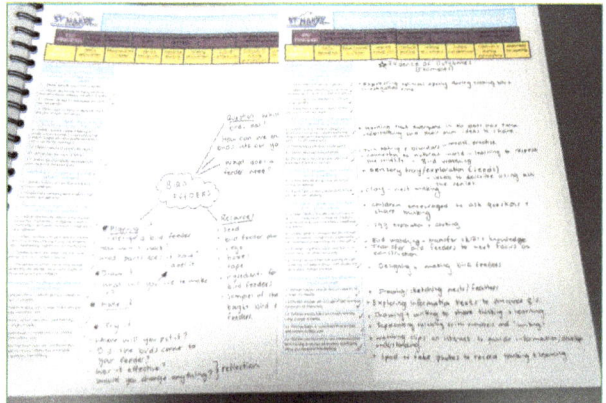

Accountability and the learning journey combined

There are two main ways of using a curriculum, defined here as a national set of standards rather than what children do each day.

1. Allow the curriculum outcomes to drive the content of your planning so that you cover them through planned activities.

2. Offer provocations for play and, as the children engage with them, consider what they have been exploring through tracking back to the outcome statements.

As children get older, the balance between child-led and adult-led planning changes. The Floorbooks allow both to occur as direct teaching of a skill or a piece of knowledge can be documented as well as the exploration of the skill in real-life situations.

In the case study that follows, the outcomes or key notes of concepts, skills or pieces of knowledge are included on the individual pages rather than collectively at the rear of the Floorbook.

Case study: What does the wind blow?

by Rebekah Garwood (Australia)

My pedagogy is based on my belief that children learn best through play and playful learning, and that early childhood environments should be rich with infinite possibilities for learning and high-play affordance. I am passionate about inquiry learning and nature-based learning, with influences from the schools of Reggio Emilia, the constructivist approach and the nature-based education movement. I feel strongly that effective learning is driven by the interests of the child and use a project or inquiry-learning approach to deliver an intentionally integrated curriculum.

To me, inquiry is about children wondering, imagining, discovering, doing and demonstrating. Children learn about the world around them, important social and emotional skills, and how to learn. In the process, they build a collective knowledge together.

Children drawing and writing together (top). Experimenting outside is documented and valued (bottom)

See, think, wonder as a frame for children's reflection

Children lead the learning. I encourage their independence, not directly answering a question but wondering with them, questioning how we might find out and constructing provocations that will enable them to take the next step.

Initial idea gathered in the Floorbook

Our inquiry learning journeys are recorded in Talking and Thinking Floorbooks, with the children and me deciding what and how to document. The Floorbooks also allow me to reflect on and map the learning and plan for 'what next' using PLODs.

We had been focusing on nature-based learning in kindergarten. On their return from a wintry school break, many children were noticing the wind. They were hearing it whistle through the

Recording observations to link to a previous experience

doors, talking about how they 'were blowed into school' and discussing the appearance of fallen branches and trees. Some were also busily making simple paper kites and planes at the writing table.

A natural inquiry was emerging. To stimulate my own thinking, I created a mind map based on the element of air and mapped out the PLODs and links to the curriculum. I then created a Talking Tub and we explored many of the elements together through a 3D mind map. This was an exciting start – the children were discussing what they knew and articulating what they wanted to know.

Throughout the inquiry we wondered, hypothesised, experimented, explored and created together. Our thinking, doing and learning were documented into our Floorbook. Children need time to go deep in their learning, yet too often projects are influenced or curtailed by time constraints, adult expectations and planning. The term was drawing to an end and my children were still highly engaged. While air and wind still featured in our work, we moved into flight and they were keen to investigate, design and build their own kites.

The Western Australian Kindergarten Curriculum Guidelines were placed into the Floorbook, with outcomes highlighted and dated as the inquiry project progressed. It was affirming to see how much learning had occurred. The

The process of kite making

children's literacy and desire to write and take control of the documentation emerged through the project, as did evidence of their maths exploration and use. I believe this is because the project was driven by their interests; it was authentic and relevant to them.

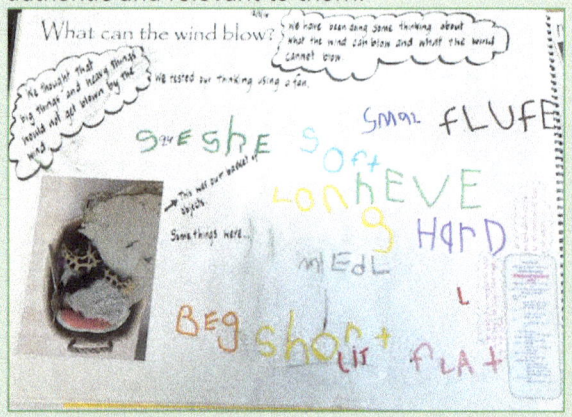

Adding curriculum links on a Floorbook page

Throughout the inquiry, I could see them become increasingly more independent as learners. They were engaged, motivated and receptive to my efforts to extend their thinking through Talking Tubs and other intentional provocations.

SECTION 2. FEATURES

By using the curriculum outcomes or quality standards to monitor breadth and balance as they are explored, the adult can check whether they are providing a balanced series of experiences and opportunities for children in their setting. The forms at the back can be linked to any document that you feel resonates with you and your setting; it may be a set of skills linked to school readiness or specific mathematics detail not held in the main curriculum.

The summary grid below provides a useful way of checking whether you have incorporated all aspects of a Floorbook and given each of them the same value. Taking time to review and audit the quality of the documentation and the planning that stems from it is an important factor in the development of high-quality provision.

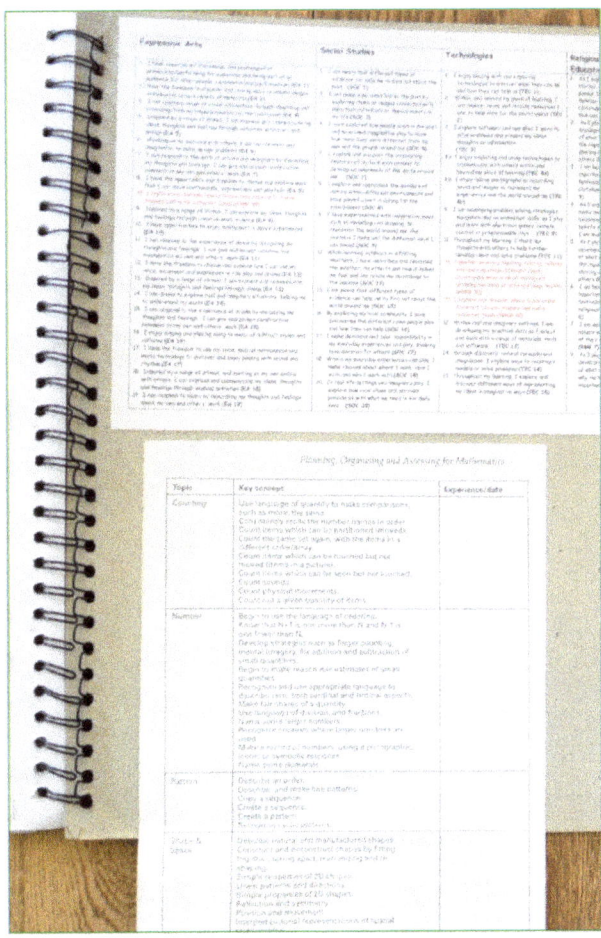

Accountability to a specific curriculum focus such as maths

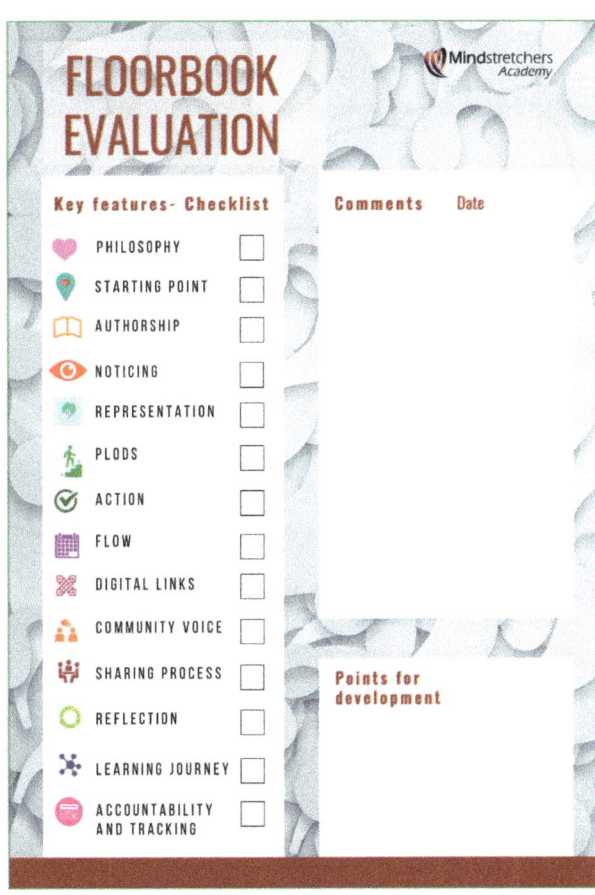

In environments that look for evidence of experience, placing the page number alongside the outcome cannot guarantee or prove that children have acquired the knowledge, skill or concept but it can indicate coverage through the planning process. The individual detail is held in our Family Books or Learning Journals, as noted in the 'Tracking flow and progression' section.

67

Section 3.
Key strategies

Four key influences shape how a learning environment structures experiences and opportunities for children: the time available, the space available, the resources available and, of course, the adult and the role they play. In this section we explore the three main strategies that research suggests make the most difference to the content of a Floorbook. The adult is pivotal in all of them and adopts slightly different roles. Joint involvement episodes (Bruner 1961) engage the adult and child in a social experience that both can discuss and reflect on.

Where the adult is using the contents of a Talking Tub, they may be engaged in what Rogoff (2003) refers to as *guided participation with others*. If the adult has an intent to teach a core skill and the child has a desire to achieve it, then the interaction aligns itself with mastery orientation (Sylva 2004, from the EPPE project). Collaboration and enrichment of a space for provocation build on the concept that children (and adults at times) are in what Lev Vygotsky referred to as the *zone of proximal development*; a transitional space between not knowing and knowing where working with others can help you to embed and apply the new skill or knowledge so that it is integrated into who you are. Talking Tubs encourage the celebration and sharing of collective knowledge; 3D mind mapping provides a guided experience that can open up possibilities outside the frame of experience of the child; and finally, questioning develops aspects of interaction.

Question marks celebrate curiosity

Talking Tubs

I am often asked why the Talking Tub box is covered in question marks. The answer lies in its use: the focus is more on the skill of questioning and inquiry than on the answers. Talking Tubs are in essence the central location for objects and images selected to stimulate thinking. Rather than being simply a display in a box, they are integral to many of the aspects of this social pedagogy. In particular, they can create a balance of opinion, offer opportunities for discussion and stimulate plans for play and learning.

A Talking Tub is full of the things of life

The desire to communicate

To foster the desire to communicate, a setting must create the fundamental aspects of a dialogic space, where the spoken word or communication is valued. When communication in all of its forms is valued and considered significant, adults often record it through writing or digital systems.

Emotional literacy is rooted in supportive and caring relationships (Joseph and Strain 2003). To act on a social environment, a child needs to be able to read both their own emotional and social cues and

SECTION 3. KEY STRATEGIES

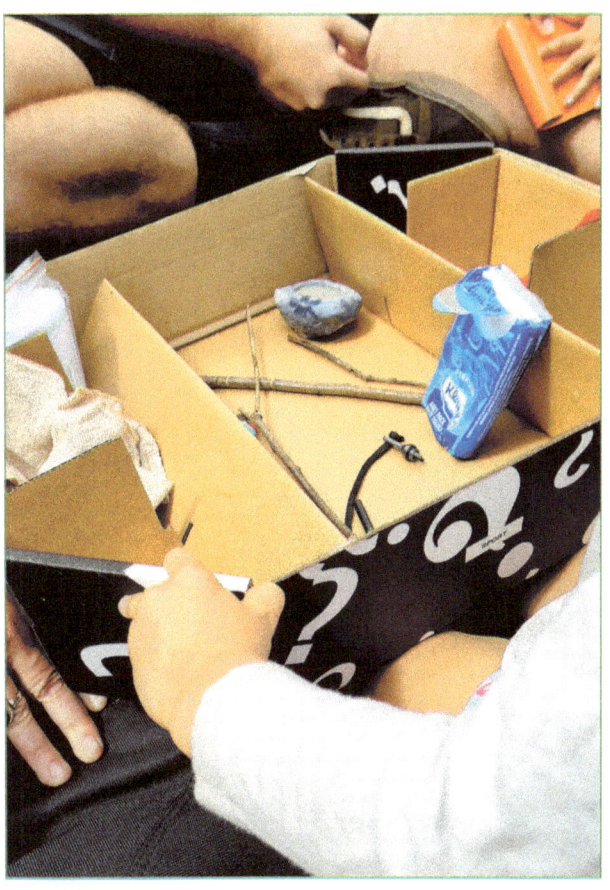

A selection of materials worthy of talk

highlighted how children's ability to code-switch their language is significant to the way that children understand what is expected of them (Cantone 2007). The use of context and objects is key to specifically supporting children in this situation.

The purpose of the Talking Tub is to expand and stimulate talk for all the children in the setting. One aspect of effective communication is understanding and developing emotional literacy.

The adult's role in this work is to narrate their own behaviours – to model language and behaviours to young children. When writing in a Floorbook, for example, we may say, 'I am feeling a bit frustrated, as I cannot remember the name of the man who came to visit.' Recalling an event through the pictures in a Floorbook allows us to use words to widen emotional literacy through noting the child's behaviour in an image in the Floorbook. For example, 'It looks like you were really curious about that worm. Do you see how closely you were looking at it?' These moments of documentation give children both a space to discuss emotions in context and the affirmation to show the progression and development of caring behaviours.

those of others. Being aware of emotional state and being able to identify it as anger, frustration or happiness, for example, have become a part of the Floorbook Approach. The ability to engage in the social construction of knowledge through engaging with others and listening to their ideas often reveals aspects of social and emotional literacy. 'Emotional literacy' is the ability to recognise, label and understand feelings in oneself and in others. As Denham (1986) and Webster-Stratton (1999) suggest, it is a prerequisite skill to emotional regulation, successful interpersonal interactions and problem-solving and so is one of the most important skills a child is taught in the early years.

If we are to consult children, we need to be able to understand their relationship with the world and therefore it is valuable if they have a sizeable vocabulary available to give opinions and emotional responses (see Table 3.1 for some examples). Substantial research suggests that children with special rights, such as physical disability (Feldman et al 1993) or low income (Eisenberg 1999), have more limited feeling vocabularies. One study has

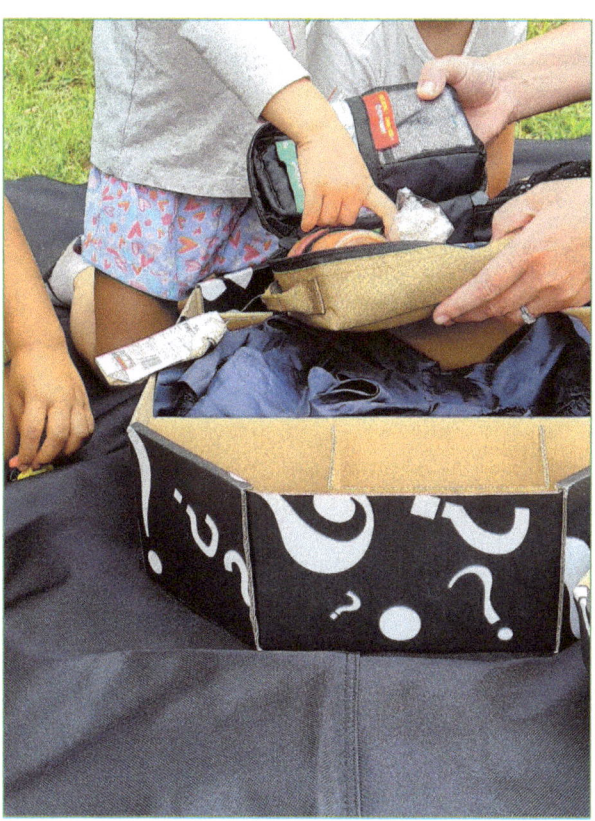

Choosing objects to explore

69

SECTION 3. KEY STRATEGIES

Table 3.1: An emotional vocabulary

Annoyed	Disgusted	Ignored	Relieved
Bored	Ecstatic	Impatient	Safe
Brave	Embarrassed	Important	Sensitive
Calm	Enjoying	Interested	Shy
Caring	Excited	Jealous	Strong
Cheerful	Fearful	Joyful	Stubborn
Clumsy	Fed-up	Lonely	Tense
Comfortable	Free	Lost	Thoughtful
Confused	Friendly	Loving	Thrilled
Cooperative	Frustrated	Overwhelmed	Troubled
Creative	Generous	Peaceful	Uncomfortable
Cruel	Gentle	Pleasant	Weary
Curious	Gloomy	Proud	Worried
Disappointed	Guilty	Relaxed	

Talking Tubs and the place of 'things'

When asked what to put into a Talking Tub, I often reply, 'stuff – the things of life'. Let me explain my thinking around this rather non-descript word 'things'. As a child, I grew up being aware of the drawer where the random things go! It is the drawer in your house where you hide away the interesting stuff that has no real defined purpose or home. The language around this is important, as it needs to convey a deeper meaning. I could use the word *provocation* or alternatively *resource* but either suggests a purchased item. I could use *artefact* but that ages the object as something culturally revered. *Tool* suggests that the item has a purpose and not all things in life really do. Or perhaps I could use the phrase *a range of objects*, yet that suggests a lack of relationship.

So I have come to enjoy the *things of life* as a phrase for these reasons.

- *Things of life* have a story, a history of people and place that can emerge in conversations around the Talking Tub.
- *Things of life* celebrate the diversity of humans as we all live in place-based experiences affected by climate, culture and community.

Engaging with real objects

SECTION 3. KEY STRATEGIES

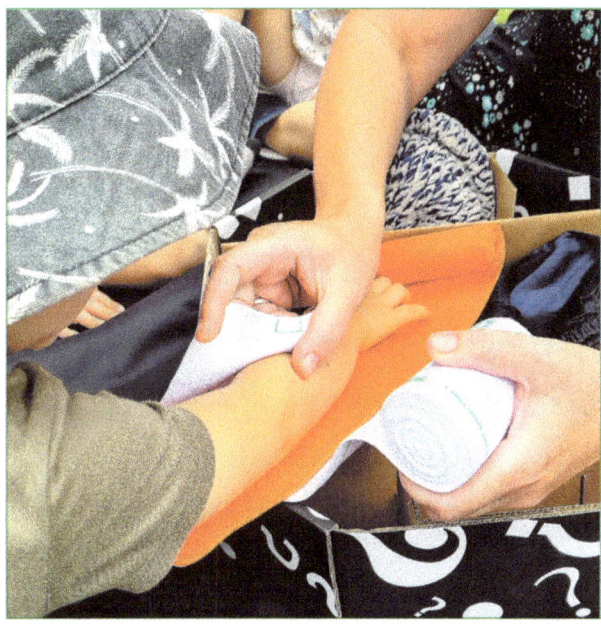

- *Things of life* can be wide and complex, from a piece of fabric to a photograph of a place, an object or a personality.
- *Things of life* can be one thing to one person and something different to another. To a child, blue fabric can be the sky, or a flower, or the colour of a pair of shoes.
- *Things of life* are commonplace and therefore accessible to everyone.

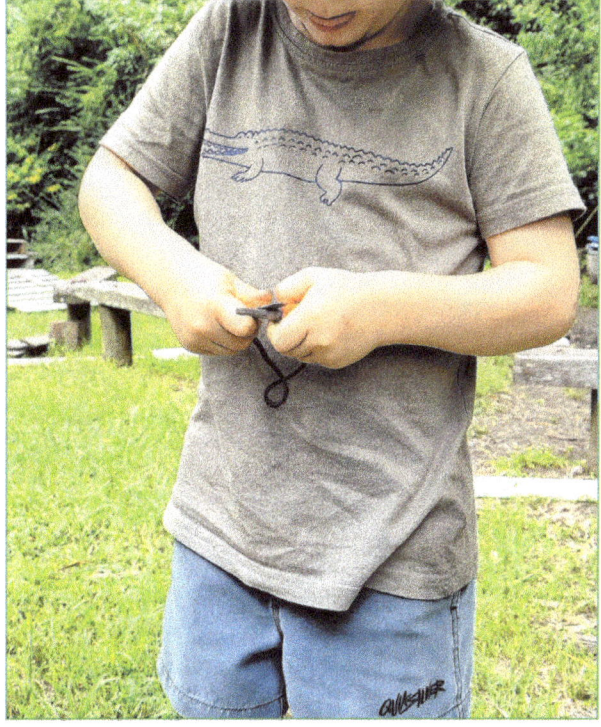

Physical engagement (top). Exploring the possibilities of objects (bottom)

- *Things of life* are relational. They link together in a mesh-like way through a myriad of different concepts. An egg can be related to a hen, an eggcup or a chick. This open nature is full of the infinite variety and affordance that encourage and support divergent thinking.

Connections

A Talking Tub links children's experiences to the new content you are exploring within the setting. The closer the contents of the Talking Tub to the child's experience, the shorter the bridge the child needs to make. For example, a conversation offers an easier link when it is about a bird they see in the backyard every day than an exotic bird they have never seen first hand. Once these links start to form, the child builds up a framework of understanding that we can then build on by developing concepts such as bird, feather and flight.

Lines of inquiry in a Talking Tub on birds

Understanding

Watching children handle objects and images from the Talking Tub is always enlightening and supports us to understand the child, their motivation and their past experiences. A Talking Tub provides a transitional space for exploring an object in multiple ways. As adults, we may have chosen to include an object such as a feather with the idea of looking at shades of colour. Yet the child may respond to it through movement, or model using it as a quill, or sort several feathers by order of size. At these

71

moments the adult needs to be attentive and knowledgeable, so that they notice and understand the potential for inquiry.

Children handling the objects (above and top right)

Preparation and organisation

Talking Tubs are structured by the adult. They are used to support interaction between the adult and child through discussion and inquiry.

The aim of providing two-dimensional images (photos and diagrams) and selecting real three-dimensional materials is to stimulate the brain to recall memories and connect to children's existing frameworks of understanding.

While several options are possible, fundamentally the sequence is normally to start from either:

- a child observation or fascination and then respond with the Talking Tub, or
- an adult need and then set up an invitation to work on an area of learning they feel needs to be explored.

Next, we consider what objects we could gather and collect that would be interesting for children.

- Don't make all the objects and images too obvious, as this will restrict thinking to only object naming. Although such thinking does have a place in language acquisition, it represents only a small part of oracy.
- Include images of the process of making things that you think the children may enjoy. This allows the adult to judge motivation at the same time as helping children see the possibilities. Accepting children's choices can be tricky when they cast aside an image that you felt inspired by, but a democratic space has no place for false consultation.
- Include images of previous groups of children in the same place. This is interesting to children as they may know older members of the families in those images and it also presents a sense of gravitas and tradition. A child holding an image once said, 'This is Gabby's boat, that is John's sister … look … she was by the stream. That is where I am going to take my boat as well.'
- Objects need to have an invitation within them that draws children to handle them. Real materials, such as maps or a compass, will be more attractive than an image of them, for all the reasons noted earlier.

Writing down what children say when they open the Tub

To make the thinking behind the objects visible to other current or future team members, a Talking Tub has a planning sheet that maps out the key lines of inquiry or main ideas that sit within the fascination. Table 3.2 present an example around sustainability.

SECTION 3. KEY STRATEGIES

Sustainable practice in *taking care of our place* may include location and mapping, properties and durability of materials, erosion and compaction of land, recycling options, and use and sources of power (the first column of the table). However, these lines of inquiry need to be explored through experiences that connect to people and place, so we may look inside a lunchbox to start the inquiry or map the children's place to talk about an issue they feel is important. The second column of the table shows how such provocations might be represented in a Talking Tub.

The third column moves a Talking Tub from a simple provocation for talking and thinking to a more intentional approach, as it can demonstrate:

- the learning behind the line of inquiry to which the adults are held accountable, such as curriculum outcomes
- support for interaction around the use of a Talking Tub by noting down some open questions or wondering questions
- a skills- and concept-driven approach
- a focus on capacities and dispositions
- schema.

The line of inquiry and the contents of the tub are set out in a grid, like the example in Table 3.2. This grid is attached to the lid of the Talking Tub, so that all staff are aware of the possibilities for thinking and learning that the creator of the tub has thought through.

Table 3.2: Example of a Talking Tub grid showing lines of inquiry and contents related to sustainability

Line of inquiry	Object or image in the Talking Tub	Links to curriculum, wonderings or knowledge, skill or concept
Location and mapping	Examples of different maps, old and new. A compass and an old phone (eg, GPS location, Google Maps). Images of areas of the site (taken by children) to discuss.	I wonder how we know where we live? How did people know where they were before we had smartphones?
Properties of materials	A range of familiar paper and plastic materials, such as a crisp packet, an old shoe, an orange skin and a yoghurt pot.	I wonder how we can test for which one stays for the longest time?
Impact on land and water	Images of footpaths where no plants grow and areas where they flourish. Animals living in odd spaces, like a shrimp in a bottle or a pigeon with an all-blue plastic nest. (Be sensitive to the level of detail in images.)	Why do you think no plants grow on the path any more? I wonder why the shrimp lived in the bottle and not under the rock?
Litter management	Images of the recycling bins and any problem areas in the setting, to offer the challenge of 'What do we do?'	If we could design a new bin, I wonder what it would look like?

continued ...

SECTION 3. KEY STRATEGIES

Table 3.2: Example of a Talking Tub grid showing lines of inquiry and contents related to sustainability (continued)

Line of inquiry	Object or image in the Talking Tub	Links to curriculum, wonderings or knowledge, skill or concept
Recycling	Images or examples of the object and what it has turned into; for example, a nylon carpet into a tray, plastic bags into a fleece jacket, paper into new cardboard containers and plates.	I wonder how we could change something here into something different?
Reuse and upcycling	Images or examples of reusing an item, such as a Wellington boot to grow flowers in, or a jam jar for a candle holder.	Looking at the images, I wonder if any give you an idea about something you might like to explore?
Water use	Plastic bottles or jars of dirty and clean water and an empty one for no water.	I wonder how we could make dirty water clean?
Transport	Bike, train, car and plane can all be represented with a range of wheels. Place them alongside various images of local transport options.	If we had four wheels, what would we make?
Energy	A range of lightbulbs, forms of torches; a real switch box and a short length of wire; a solar-powered toy, a battery, an image of a windmill.	How does the bulb light up? I wonder how we could test these to see if they have any energy?
Food consumption	Small food examples in images and real state. Bag of soil. Images of organisms, such as worms.	I wonder how an apple changes into soil?

Once the team has created the contents for a tub, it can store them in the setting in a wallet or tub as many fascinations re-emerge over a year, especially those linked to concepts.

The first sessions will use a Talking Tub with one or two items linked to the lines of inquiry. Then, as the educator notices where the children's interest lies, they take out the original objects and add more to expand the inquiry the children want to explore.

The contents of a Talking Tub therefore change throughout the inquiry. With children adding more materials and adults taking out and replacing articles, it stays interesting and responsive.

If we take any one of the lines of inquiry set out in Table 3.2, we can make a second Talking Tub just about that line of inquiry. Doing this allows the inquiry to go in-depth, so the focus becomes slow, deep learning rather than touching on many things for a very short period. So, for a bird inquiry, we could just explore beaks or feet, or children may have a fascination with feathers. The Talking Tub allows the educator to reframe and deepen a sense of fascination and curiosity. Without making decisions about the line of inquiry, they shape and influence ideas through the context and objects presented in the Talking Tub.

SECTION 3. KEY STRATEGIES

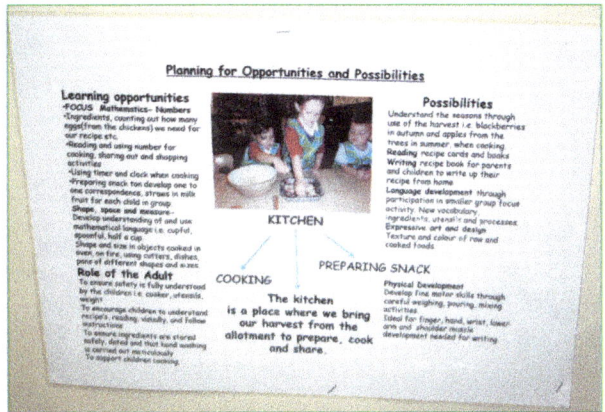

PLODs and possibilities

Not everything goes through a Talking Tub, but it can offer some possibilities to children in a well-framed way. The photo above shows how posters can support educators to see the PLODs and possibilities that emerge from areas of play that could be the focus at a group time with a Talking Tub.

3D mind mapping

Mind mapping was made popular by Tony Buzan and his work on creating concept maps. A mind map (or brainstorm/spider diagram) is a visual thinking tool used to capture information and ideas. It begins with a central idea (the topic to be explored) and branches out into key themes as ideas develop further, radiating from the centre out.

Three-dimensional mind mapping is much more fluid, responsive and engaging for children. The key themes are the lines of inquiry that either the adult or the child identifies.

One effective way of using Talking Tubs is to create a Talkaround Time with children and discuss the connections between the objects. For example, further to the sustainability scenario in the Talking Tubs section above, the children may place the crisp packet next to the wellies. The adult's role in the interaction is to support them to talk about the link. It may be that a child puts their boots on to go to the recycling centre or that they love cheesy crisps. The important part is to celebrate the relationship between the child and the things of life. This supports oracy and will develop divergent thinking and concept-based problem-solving.

A Talking Tub is framed around adult lines of inquiry but children's ideas and lines of inquiry can emerge from the mind-mapping session.

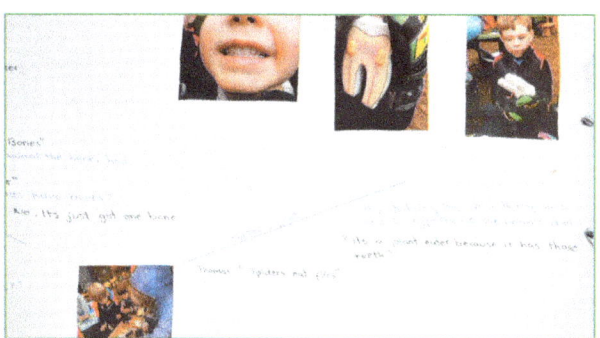

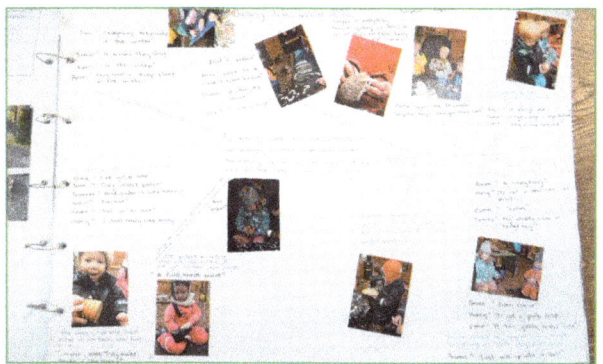

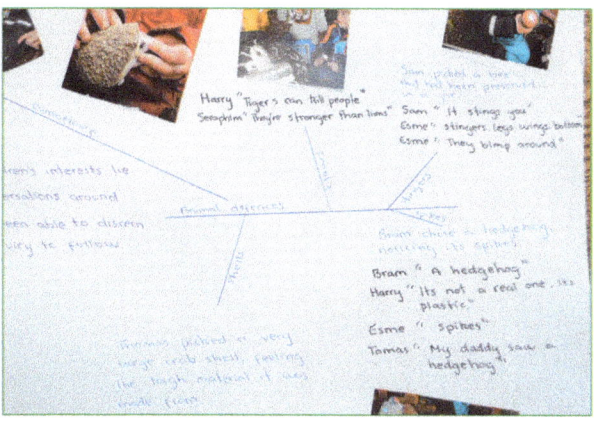

Noting down the children's mind mapping through Talkaround Time

Lines of inquiry from children

SECTION 3. KEY STRATEGIES

The adult may write a word on the yellow strip to denote a line of inquiry and narrow the focus, or may open up the conversation to listen to what the children will bring up.

The strips of yellow paper used for mind mapping are designed to:

- make the ideas visually bold for those children who need visual support
- be flexible, in that the ideas can be moved around and new mind maps created

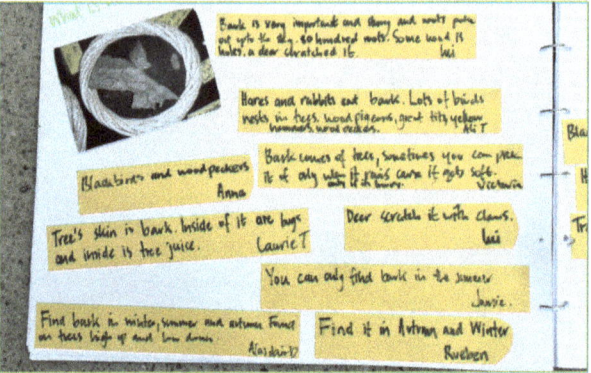

Digging down into one aspect of the inquiry

- be shared in a Floorbook, as they hold the lines of inquiry from the children (and then specific PLODs can be written beside them)

Mind map on what a tree is

- use the photographs (along with a clear black pen) to document the mind-mapping session effectively. This image is then added to the Floorbook to share the process.

3D mind mapping is an effective way of working with children on any subject as it allows them to clearly see the objects and images and how they connect to create meaning.

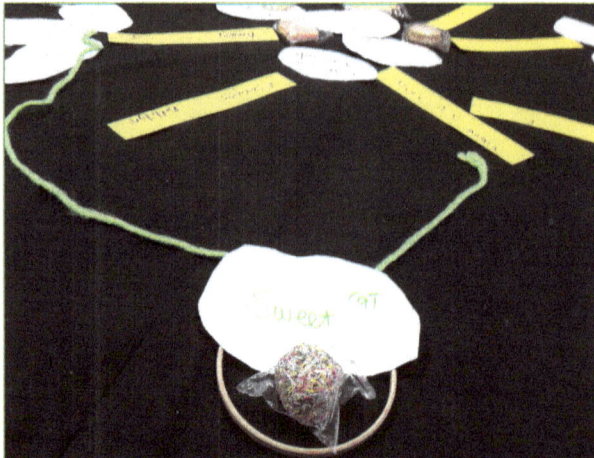

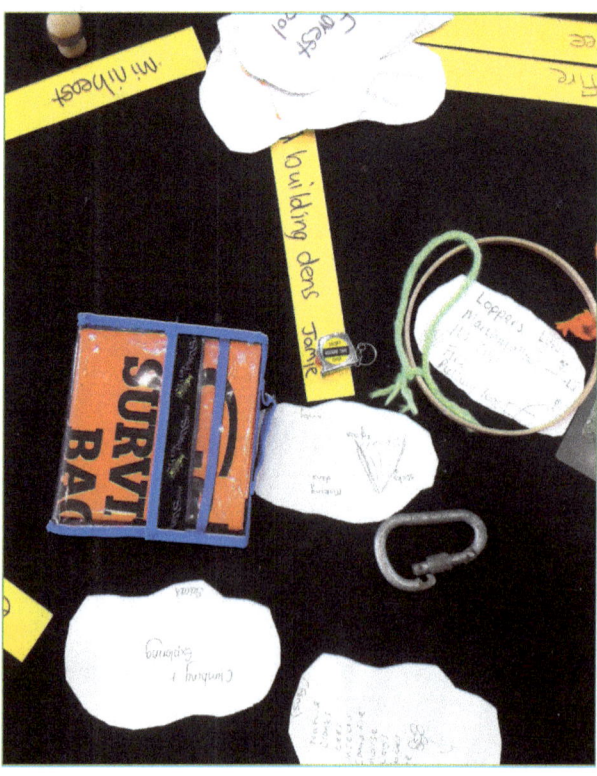

3D mind maps on healthy eating (top and middle) and on risk assessment with children (bottom)

Questioning

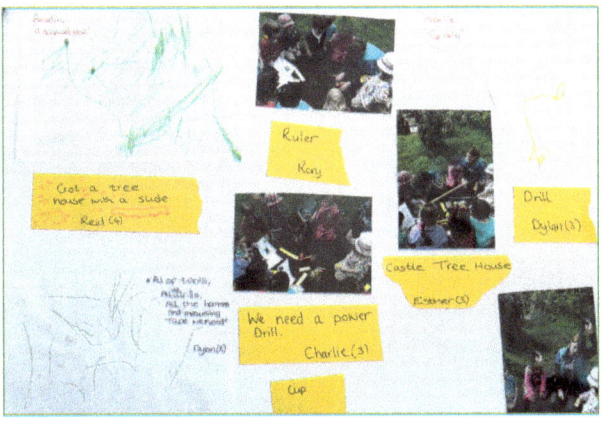

Adult interaction

When we consult children about what they know, we need to embrace that their life experiences and their forms of communication are diverse. Further, given we work with groups of children, we have to accept that we respond to their broad fascinations, while monitoring that dominant children do not always drive our planning. All children need to have an adult to listen to them and a time to communicate their thoughts but often we adults fill the space. For every one question we ask, we should make seven affirmations – such as eye contact, a nod, a smile or whatever you feel comfortable doing – to offer space for children to think. Speech and language specialists recommend that we wait at least seven seconds for a response to a question.

We can use discussion *and* questioning to provoke thinking; however, discussion is often more effective in creating a deeper level of thinking.

Noting questions that emerge in a Floorbook

The following kinds of questions encourage children to think more deeply (Lipman 1988; Wilks 1995):

- closed and open questions in adult interactions
- meta-cognitive questions, which focus on the learner's awareness, evaluation and regulation of their own thinking
- reflective questions, which engage the learner or thinker in deliberate, purposeful consideration of the effectiveness of actions and experiences.

Adults have an impact on the experiences of children through their interactions. One way to interact is to ask each other questions.

First you need to establish the foundational understanding of what type of question you are asking. There are, in essence, two kinds of questions: closed questions, which can be answered with a *yes* or *no*, and open questions, which encourage the person to expand on what they were thinking. For example:

- **Closed question:** *Do you like flowers?* This question can be answered with a *yes* or *no*.

- **Open questions:**
  What do you think about flowers? This question requires a more complex answer.
  If the flower could talk, what would it say? This question moves into a more philosophical way of thinking.

Adult using open-ended questions

SECTION 3. KEY STRATEGIES

Possibility thinking

Possibilities are generated by children (and adults) in all areas of learning, including imaginative play, musical exploration and composition, cooking, mark-making and writing, outdoor physical play, mathematical development and early scientific inquiry. Possibility thinking is the means by which questions are asked or puzzles are surfaced – through multiple ways of generating the question 'What if …?' (Craft 2000, 2001, 2002). Children may experience 'What if …?' subconsciously in the flow of engagement. For example, a two-year-old may realise that, in crawling through the long grass, they start to make a 'track'; an eight-year-old may realise that they can make a number pattern by following the 9 times table; or a pair of three-year-olds may make 'soup' from daisy petals.

Possibility thinking essentially involves a transition in understanding. In other words, it shifts from 'What is this?' to exploration – for example, 'What can I/we do with this?' Fostering possibility thinking involves enabling children to find and refine problems, as well as to solve them. Studies in primary classrooms have explored this distinction between finding and solving problems (Jeffrey 2004, 2005; Jeffrey and Craft 2004).

Environments that invite curiosity

Creative thinking

Bruce (2004) argues that, without sensitive engagement with young children and their families, 'emergent possibilities for creativity that are in every child do not develop or can be quickly extinguished' (p 12). An equally compelling case can be made for the way we work with older children. Adults in early years settings have opportunities to develop practice to foster children's creativity, focusing on each child's motivations and interests and, in valuing and appreciating these, encouraging exploration without 'invading the child's creative idea or taking it over' (Bruce 2004, p 25).

Floorbooks support and nourish creative thinking as an approach, embracing the individual within the group, celebrating the complexity and variability of the natural world as their context.

The value of Floorbooks in higher-order thinking

The Floorbook Approach focuses on the learning dispositions to develop higher-order thinking in environments that give children 'space', in a metaphorical sense, to contribute their voice and their ideas to the learning environment. In this space, children:

- are actively involved in their learning to increase motivation and empowerment
- persist when situations or activities are difficult or uncertain
- have the opportunity to communicate with others in complex ways
- take responsibility for their own learning and how to share it.

Higher-order thinking models

Several approaches to developing higher-order thinking – that is, pulling a concept apart and discussing its various aspects – are possible. Floorbooks make this process of thinking, with all of its inherent challenges, problems and failures, very clear. In this way, just like the first Floorbook on electrical understanding with four-year-olds (see 'History of Floorbooks' in Section 1), we can embrace the vast range of ways that children think about the world. We can use these ideas around higher-order thinking to support progression in our work with young children.

Bloom's Taxonomy is a hierarchy of thinking processes that we can use at the front of a Floorbook as a guide and reminder to adults in considering interactions. How often do we focus on memory recall rather than on developing hypotheses through applying a new aspect of knowledge or exploring a concept?

While it is a useful reminder of the complexity of thinking, Bloom's has recently been challenged as being too hierarchical, given children operate on a range of levels at any one time. Yet the general understanding of the layers of thinking it offers remains valuable when we link it to the understanding of the vocabulary we use in our interactions with children. Do we use questions that stem from knowledge, such as *What is that called?* or do we use questions from an evaluative standpoint, such as *How do you feel about that?* Table 3.3 lists the thinking skills along with the words we tend to use in our interactions with children that make a difference. It also notes question stems because they can trigger your own awareness of how you use questions in your practice.

Table 3.3: Adaptation of Bloom's Taxonomy

Thinking skill (increasing from remembering to creativity)	Key words	Question stems
Remember Can the child remember information?	Name, list, describe, relate, write, copy, search, recall, label, match	What happened after …? How many …? Who was that? Can you tell me why? What is …?
Understand Can the child explain ideas or concepts?	Outline, compare, order, identify	Can you write that in your own words? What could happen next? Who do you think …?
Apply Can the child use the information in a new way?	Solve, show, report, develop, share	Do you have another example where …? Could you make a model to show what you know?
Analyse Can the child see the differences?	Examine, compare, contrast, explain, analyse	How is … similar to …? Why did that happen?
Evaluate Can the child talk about their decisions?	Choose, decide, justify, evaluate	How did you feel about that? What do you think?
Create Can the child create new ideas and make items?	Create, design, construct, imagine, devise	Can you design a …? How could you …?

Section 4.
Breadth, balance and accountability

While every country has its own way of presenting the planning process, most present it as a single cycle. Yet that process should perhaps be a series of loops that go off in a range of directions (Leggo 2007). We know from research that learning is not a standard, straight route from start to finish and in reality we would do well to consider how we can create a planning and documentation process that can make that complexity visible. Floorbooks go a long way to achieving that reality.

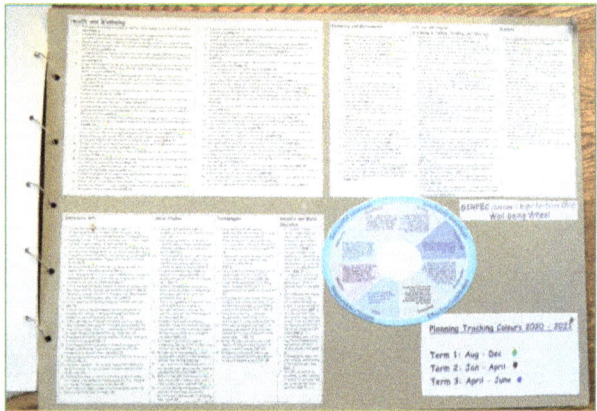

Curriculum outcomes

Principles that underpin curricula

The word *curriculum* has various interpretations around the world. Some curricula describe what experiences children have every day, while others represent a set of norms, usually laid out in experiences and outcomes, and are often associated with expected milestones in children's development. The following two examples illustrate contrasting approaches.

- 'An effective curriculum is a holistic and ambitious plan that sets out what you intend children in your setting to learn and experience across all seven areas of learning. It will be tailored to the age group(s) you work with and should be ambitious for all children.' (Department for Education, England, no date)
- 'The early childhood curriculum ... values children, recognising them as full of potential from birth ... [and] is also about **what** the child wants to learn within a caring, nurturing environment' (Education Scotland 2020, p 52).

Definitions change further as children enter the school system, where the term tends to be used more in relation to learning areas or subjects.

What curricula have in common is that they are set out by a body of people, whether that is a government or another group.

You can tell a lot about a country and its view of education by going to the principles; the foundations on which the curriculum was created. Let us consider how we address the issues of curriculum accountability generally through Floorbooks.

Challenge and enjoyment

Children and young people should find their learning challenging, engaging and motivating. To this end, Floorbooks elevate the child's voice so that it drives the learning journey. The curriculum should encourage high aspirations and ambitions for all and the open-ended nature of a Floorbook allows children's thinking to extend to its full potential, rather than restricting it to age categories.

Breadth

All children and young people should have the opportunity for a broad range of experiences that create a foundation for further learning. Their learning should be planned with intent and organised so that they will learn and develop through a variety of contexts within both the setting and other aspects of school life.

Progression

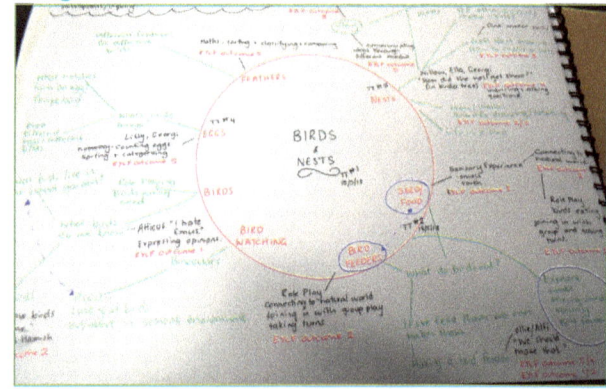

Learning journey linked to the curriculum

Each stage of learning should build on earlier knowledge and achievements, rather than being limited by the age of a child. Floorbooks share progression as a group while providing individual evidence held in the Family Books or portfolios. Each child is encouraged to contribute in any way that they feel they can, which may mean, for example that a four-year-old is exploring a similar concept to a three-year-old.

Depth

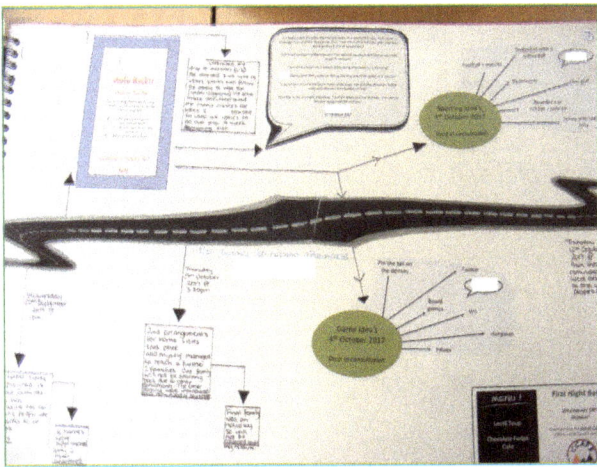

Planning programmes and actions as a team

Floorbooks make highly visible the opportunities for children and young people to develop their full capacity for different types of thinking and learning, exploring and achieving more advanced levels of understanding. The slowness of this work encourages depth of thinking and the evidence within the documentation is often used to justify that professional decision.

Personalisation and choice

When a child is seen as agentic, the learning planned for children and young people can more readily respond to their individual needs and support aptitudes and talents. A divergent approach provides opportunities for exercising personal choice that can support empowerment in a wide range of areas of learning.

Coherence – 'links'

The experiences and opportunities of children and young people should combine to form a coherent, holistic journey. In environments where discrete subjects are explored, there should be clear links to bring together different strands between home and setting.

Relevance

When children see the value of what they are learning and its relevance to their present and future lives, it may feel more relevant. Imagine a child experiencing white paint to represent milk and contrast that with actually drinking a glass of milk or looking at a cow. The latter experiences are real-world and authentic and a Floorbook works very effectively to capture them as it shares imagery taken inside, outside and beyond the gate into the local community.

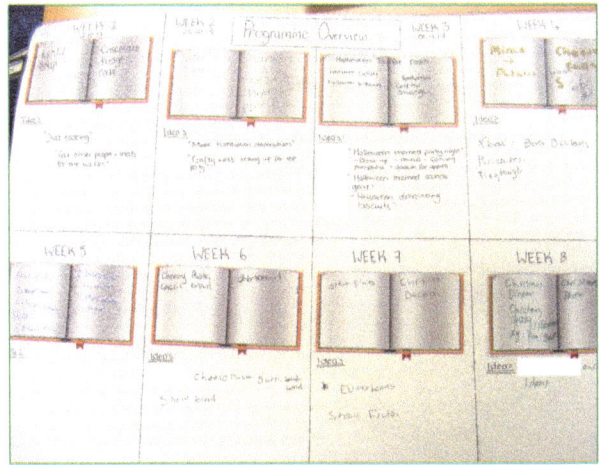

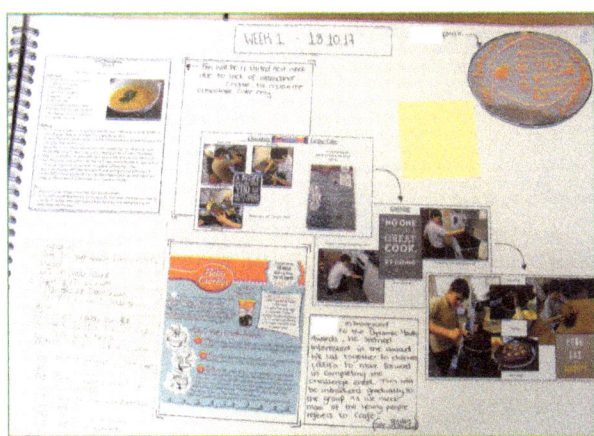

Working with parents

SECTION 4. BREADTH, BALANCE AND ACCOUNTABILITY

How Floorbooks support the curriculum – England and Northern Ireland

The EYFS has four guiding principles to shape practice in early years settings.

- Every child is a **unique child**, who is constantly learning and can be resilient, capable, confident and self-assured.
- Children learn to be strong and independent through **positive relationships**.
- Children learn and develop well in **enabling environments with teaching and support** from adults, who respond to their individual interests and needs and help them to build their learning over time. Children benefit from a strong partnership between practitioners and parents and/or carers.
- **Learning and development** are important – children develop and learn at different rates (Department for Education, England 2025, p 7).

The EYFS learning and development requirements consist of three main areas.

1. The seven **educational programmes**, or areas of learning and development, are made up of:
   - three prime areas: communication and language; physical development; and personal, social and emotional development
   - four specific areas: literacy; mathematics; understanding the world; and expressive arts and design.
2. The **early learning goals** summarise the knowledge, skills and understanding that all young children should have gained by the end of the reception year.
3. The **assessment requirements** specify when and how practitioners must assess children's achievements, and when and how they should discuss children's progress with parents and/or carers.

The table below details how the principles are reflected in the Floorbook Approach.

Principle	How the Floorbook Approach demonstrates it
Unique child	Floorbooks are inclusive and create a balance of decision-making between the adult and the child. Children share what they say, do, make and write in the Floorbook as different ways of knowing that celebrate the individual within the community of their group. The Floorbook makes visible and values perseverance, tenacity and failure. It demonstrates respect through the care and attention it gives to children's voices and representing them well. In this way, children can feel empowered and develop a strong sense of agency that supports them to be successful on a complex, challenging and creative learning journey.
Positive relationships	Floorbooks embrace diverse ways of contributing what you know and think. They value and make visible all the people they come into contact with, including families, children and visitors from the community. They display multiple ways of knowing and celebrate communication in its widest form, helping children realise what effective communication looks like and how it works in a real context. This further supports children to understand how we develop positive relationships in acquiring skills, knowledge and understanding of the world around us.

continued ...

Principle	How the Floorbook Approach demonstrates it
Enabling environment	Through the flexible and responsive inquiry approach of Floorbooks, which welcomes diversity over conformity, children's learning is holistic and meaningful. This environment embraces individuality within a community of learning. Although of course curriculum outcomes feature in the work of practitioners, the voice of children must always lead the way as this supports them to develop agency and confidence. This approach keeps children's interests and needs at the forefront of the provision.
Learning and development	The co-constructed approach of the Floorbook shows shared, democratic decision-making, even to the level of using voting systems. The physicality of the Talking Tub supports every child's right to be heard. Further, documenting learning with and for children in the Floorbook creates a collaborative space for all children and their families. Including many languages, forms of knowledge and perspectives in approaching a task or event supports children to develop tolerance and to celebrate diversity. Four aspects valued throughout the Floorbook are the child, the practitioner, the family and the community. It provides a tangible way of sharing acts of citizenship.

Planning

In planning and guiding what children learn, practitioners must reflect on the different rates at which children are developing and adjust their practice appropriately. Three characteristics of effective teaching and learning are:

- playing and exploring – children investigate and experience things, and 'have a go'
- active learning – children concentrate and keep on trying if they encounter difficulties, and enjoy achievements
- creating and thinking critically – children develop their own ideas, make links between them and develop strategies for doing things (Department for Education, England 2025, p 17).

The Floorbooks are effective as they empower children's thinking and elevate their agency and activism so that children learn by leading their own play, as well as by taking part in play guided by adults. Practitioners get the content of that form of responsive planning through looking back at the pages of the Floorbook during planning times.

To stimulate children's interests, practitioners respond to each child's emerging needs and guide their development through warm, positive interactions. In this way, children can both learn in a social group situation and have personal records that enable them to progress. (In the Floorbook Approach, these records are called Family Books or Learning Journals, not portfolios.)

Practitioners use assessment to find out about what children know and can do, what interests them, how they are progressing, what new learning opportunities are presented and what additional support they may need. This style of formative assessment is the central idea within the documentation of children's thinking. It allows us to then match what children know, can do and are fascinated by to the experiences we provide and the support we offer.

Placing the principles, areas of learning and development and the goals of a national curriculum in the back of the Floorbooks supports everyone to keep in mind the whole picture. Practitioners can mark off the outcomes as they cover them, true to the principles of the EYFS.

How Floorbooks support the curriculum – Scotland

A young child's development often involves repetition and cycles of actions and interactions. As a starting point, research with young children supports the view that the following dimensions are among the most important aspects of child development, underpinning not just learning but also essential for survival and flourishing: **executive function and self-regulation, communication and language, confidence, creativity and curiosity, movement and coordination, and self and social development**. (Education Scotland 2020, p 23; original emphasis)

Realising the Ambition – Being Me explores what babies, toddlers and young children need in experiences, interactions and spaces both inside and outside. It offers three areas as a lens through which to support thinking:

- wellbeing (including self, social, emotional and communication)
- movement and coordination
- confidence, creativity and curiosity.

As the child's play becomes more complex, practitioners should facilitate learning through a cyclical process of responsive and intentional planning. That includes observations, interpretation and documentation of learning, responsive and intentional planning and facilitation (Education Scotland 2020, p 47).

Responsive and intentional planning guides us to consider sensitive interactions and flexible experiences with reference to children's **actions, emotions and words**. When we listen with both our heart and our ears, we come to understand what children are exploring and then we can change the environment or keep it the same to reinforce and consolidate learning.

In Scotland, curriculum guidance spans both the ELC sector and the early stages of primary school to create a seamless journey for children in relation to the pedagogical principles. The Curriculum for Excellence 'early level' is intended to support the implementation of a responsive, continuous play-based curriculum for children aged three to six years. Its emphasis is on the knowledge, skills and attributes they need to adapt, think critically and flourish in today's world.

Curriculum is defined as the totality of all that is planned for children and young people from early learning and childcare, through school and beyond. That totality can be planned for and experienced by learners across four contexts:

- curriculum areas and subjects
- interdisciplinary learning
- ethos and life of the school
- opportunities for personal achievement.

Across these four contexts, the Curriculum for Excellence supports the development of skills, attributes and dispositions for a future in a changing world. The dispositions emerge when children have a sense of empowerment and agency, yet it can be challenging to make visible all aspects of these behaviours. A Floorbook makes it possible to share all of these dispositions as it values failure and tenacity as much as joy, motivation and attainment.

continued ...

SECTION 4. BREADTH, BALANCE AND ACCOUNTABILITY

Realising the Ambition – Being Me states that:

> From a very early age children are capable of leading their own learning. As pedagogical leaders, it is our responsibility to recognise this and give children opportunities to influence **how** and **what** they want to learn. (Education Scotland 2020, p 53; original emphasis)

The table below describes how Floorbooks can contribute to meaningful curriculum experiences supporting all four capacities in the Curriculum for Excellence.

Capacity	How the Floorbook Approach demonstrates it
Successful learners	Floorbooks are inclusive and create a balance of decision-making between the adult and the child. A Floorbook makes visible and values perseverance, tenacity and failure. It demonstrates respect through the care and attention it gives to children's voices and representing them well. In this way, children can feel empowered and develop a strong sense of agency that supports them to be successful on a complex, challenging and creative learning journey.
Confident individuals	Through the flexible and responsive inquiry approach of Floorbooks, which welcomes diversity over conformity, children's learning is holistic and meaningful. This environment embraces individuality within a community of learning. Children share what they say, do, make and write in Floorbooks as different ways of knowing. Although of course curriculum outcomes feature in the work of practitioners, the voice of children must always lead the way as this supports them to develop agency and confidence.
Responsible citizens	The co-constructed approach of the Floorbook shows shared, democratic decision-making, even to the level of using voting systems. The physicality of the Talking Tub supports every child's right to be heard. Further, documenting learning with and for children in the Floorbook creates a collaborative space for all children and their families. Including many languages, forms of knowledge and perspectives of a task or event supports children to develop tolerance and to celebrate diversity. Four aspects valued throughout the Floorbook are the child, the practitioner, the family and the community. It provides a tangible way of sharing acts of citizenship.
Effective contributors	Floorbooks embrace diverse ways of contributing what you know and think. These many different forms of sharing help children realise what effective communication looks like and how it works in a real context. The planning in the Floorbook is interdisciplinary from the first moment that was documented to the point that the fascination fades away. As it crosses subject boundaries, it supports holistic inquiry.

Practitioners use assessment to find out about what children know and can do, what interests them, how they are progressing, what new learning opportunities are presented and where additional support may be required. This style of formative assessment is the central idea within the documentation of children's thinking. In this way we can then match what children know, can do and are fascinated by to the experiences we provide and the support we offer.

Placing the principles, areas of learning and development and the goals of a national curriculum in the back of the Floorbook supports everyone to keep in mind the whole picture. Practitioners can mark off the outcomes as they cover them, supporting the capacities of the Curriculum for Excellence.

SECTION 4. BREADTH, BALANCE AND ACCOUNTABILITY

How Floorbooks support the curriculum – Wales

Four purposes are the fundamental drivers for the Curriculum for Wales 2022 (Welsh Government 2024). The aim is for all children in Wales to develop as:

- ambitious, capable learners
- enterprising, creative contributors
- ethical, informed citizens
- healthy, confident individuals.

The development of these capacities will occur for infants at the start of their learning journey in the areas of:

- belonging
- communication
- exploration
- physical development
- wellbeing.

As children get older, six areas of learning become more prevalent:

- expressive arts
- health and wellbeing
- humanities
- languages, literacy and communication
- mathematics and numeracy
- science and technology.

The concept of **enabling** refers to the role of the adult, learning experiences and the environment, both inside and outside. Part of the process of enabling is to create a child-centred observation, documentation and planning process, of the kind shared in Floorbooks. The dual-language expectation in the Welsh curriculum works well within the context of the Talking Tub as it provides a provocation of language modelling, acquisition and reinforcement.

The table below describes how Floorbooks can contribute to meaningful curriculum experiences supporting all four purposes in the Welsh curriculum.

Purpose	How the Floorbook Approach demonstrates it
Ambitious, capable learners	Floorbooks are inclusive and create a balance of decision-making between the adult and the child. A Floorbook makes visible and values perseverance, tenacity and failure. It demonstrates respect through the care and attention it gives to children's voices and representing them well. In this way, children can feel empowered and develop a strong sense of agency that supports them to be successful on a complex, challenging and creative learning journey.

continued ...

SECTION 4. BREADTH, BALANCE AND ACCOUNTABILITY

Purpose	How the Floorbook Approach demonstrates it
Healthy, confident individuals	Through the flexible and responsive inquiry approach of Floorbooks, which welcomes diversity over conformity, children's learning is holistic and meaningful. This environment embraces individuality within a community of learning. Children share what they say, do, make and write in the Floorbook as different ways of knowing that celebrate the individual within the community of their group. Although of course curriculum outcomes feature in the work of practitioners, the voice of children must always lead the way as this supports them to develop agency and confidence.
Ethical, informed citizens	The co-constructed approach of the Floorbook shows shared, democratic decision-making, even to the level of using voting systems. The physicality of the Talking Tub supports every child's right to be heard. Further, documenting learning with and for children in the Floorbook creates a collaborative space for all children and their families. Including many languages, forms of knowledge and perspectives of a task or event supports children to develop tolerance and to celebrate diversity. Four aspects valued throughout the Floorbook are the child, the practitioner, the family and the community. It provides a tangible way of sharing acts of citizenship.
Enterprising, creative contributors	Floorbooks embrace diverse ways of contributing what you know and think. They display multiple ways of knowing, helping children realise what effective communication looks like and how it works in a real context. The planning in the Floorbook is interdisciplinary from the first moment that was documented to the point that the fascination fades away. As it crosses subject boundaries, it supports holistic inquiry.

Practitioners use assessment to find out about what children know and can do, what interests them, how they are progressing, what new learning opportunities are presented and where additional support may be required. This style of formative assessment is the central idea within the documentation of children's thinking. In this way we can then match what children know, can do and are fascinated by to the experiences we provide and the support we offer. The summative assessment allows adults to get a picture of what children know and can do at key points in the learning journey.

Fundamental support from Floorbooks for each curriculum

Consider these ways in which Floorbooks support every early years curriculum in the UK.

- **Breadth:** Children engage in a greater range of experiences and contexts for learning that the pages of the Floorbook make visible.
- **Depth:** Children go further in their inquiry and gain deeper understanding when we start from what they know and allow them time to research and explore. Dating the Floorbook makes visible this intentional, slow learning.
- **Progression:** Building on what children know already in the first few pages and then providing provocations through the Talking Tub extends learning. Through page numbering and dating, we can monitor progression over time during the inquiry and record the sequence of the journey.
- **Challenge and enjoyment:** Children are engaged through their own curiosity, using real resources and taking responsibility for sharing what they think and know. Celebration of failure allows children to enjoy solving problems and lead and develop their passion for learning.
- **Relevance:** The images and objects in the Talking Tub and the pages of the Floorbook connect with and reflect the children's lives, interests and cultures.
- **Coherence:** Floorbooks help children to make connections in their learning through 2D and 3D mind mapping. A Floorbook centres the inquiry on real-life contexts that help children make sense of and apply their learning to new events, which are then shared in the same Floorbook.
- **Personalisation and choice:** We can only tailor provision to meet individual needs and interests when we consult children. Having meetings, gatherings and conversations are all ways of supporting children to make choices and share their perspectives – and all of them have a place in the Floorbook.

Encouraging personalisation and choice – a Floorbook documents meetings and conversations in which children share their perspectives

SECTION 4. BREADTH, BALANCE AND ACCOUNTABILITY

The planning cycle

To be intentional in the way that children encounter a curriculum, we follow a planning cycle. One of the key features of using the Floorbook Approach in planning with and for children is that it operates as both a documentation tool and a planning tool. This section explores each aspect of the inquiry process in turn and discusses why it is significant when planning with and for children. For each aspect, this discussion is followed by questions to help you reflect on your current practice. It is important to be as reflexive as possible and ask yourself where the power lies in your environment when it comes to taking the lead in planning.

Plan made with a mind map

The key to the use of a Floorbook as a planning document lies within the planning cycle. When we plan, we enter a cycle that supports us to reflect on our practice so that our intentional actions meet the needs of children. The reflective educator enables children's ideas and plans to emerge in the process of taking action, rather than providing purely adult-led, closed, activity-based programming. A Floorbook contains the child voice and behaviours, the staff interpretation and analysis of those actions and then a response to deepen learning.

Floorbooks, Talking Tubs and the planning cycle

Collect information through noticing what children do, say, write or make

- Collect information from discussions around the Talking Tub, to build up an assessment of what children already know.
- To contextualise the planning, on the inside front cover note down the observation that started the journey.
- Transfer observation notes and the voices of the children from the staff notepads to the Floorbook.
- Film or audio-record conversations and create a link through a QR code to a secure website.
- Create a QR code to link a blog site, digital film or photo show to the physical point in the book that it relates to.
- Collect photographs taken by children and staff. Cut these out and put them in the book with drawings and diagrams created at Talkaround Time or within the main play session.

Analyse and reflect on what has been collected

- The adults bring their group Floorbooks to the planning meeting so that decisions are made on evidence, not memory.
- Look at the Floorbooks and question the experiences from many angles, noting on the pages the thoughts of the team.
- Some moments are expanded and written up in the individual profiles in a learning stories format (Carr and Lee 2012) or Family Books (Warden 2015).

SECTION 4. BREADTH, BALANCE AND ACCOUNTABILITY

- Over time, enter what children say, make, do or write, as a way of demonstrating the reflection process of staff, children and parents/carers. By dating all the comments as we enter them, we can see how often we revisit ideas.
- Put the Floorbooks on display so that children and families can revisit and reflect.
- Children and adults can choose to put aspects into their personal Learning Journals for individual evidence.

Plan

- Ask yourself if the experience you are considering is worth doing. How does it add value and depth to the learning journey?
- Do your own research if children are exploring a line of inquiry that you have limited knowledge of, such as the anatomy of a spider's mouth-parts!
- Write PLODs with clear learning – eg, Do this … to learn/explore this – on the page in a defined area so colleagues can see it easily.
- If required, select one of these PLODs and enter it in your planning diary so that everyone is aware of the line of inquiry and the experience you are offering.
- Ask children what they feel their next steps are and then note PLODs into the Floorbook with each child's name, so that you can remember when you revisit the Floorbook.

Act or do

- Identify the PLODs that have actually taken place by ticking and dating them on the Floorbook page as they occur.
- Create a cumulative mind map of the learning journey at the back of the book with the lines of inquiry and the detailed PLODs that have been covered.
- Put a page number or a date by the PLODs on the mind map to allow cross-reference back to the page of evidence in the Floorbook.

- Children and adults stick in photographs of the process of play, the thinking moments, and the challenges and failures to acknowledge the capacity of perseverance.
- Collate ideas from children collected through the consultation boards, Thinking Tree and Talking Tubs and write them in the Floorbook as PLODs.
- Create the Floorbook with the children as an integral part of the action phase so that they see the positive aspects of documentation and thinking about learning is part of an active learning/play space.

Planning diaries and Floorbooks

The specific content to share with the team can be collated into a planning diary; the principles, goals and outcomes are included for ease of reference. The icons in the following discussion represent the sections used to guide the process of planning and include questions to support educators in their practice. Section 2 noted two areas that directly link to the features of a Floorbook – PLODs and lines of inquiry – to ensure that the whole approach links together to be holistic.

Planning diary

SECTION 4. BREADTH, BALANCE AND ACCOUNTABILITY

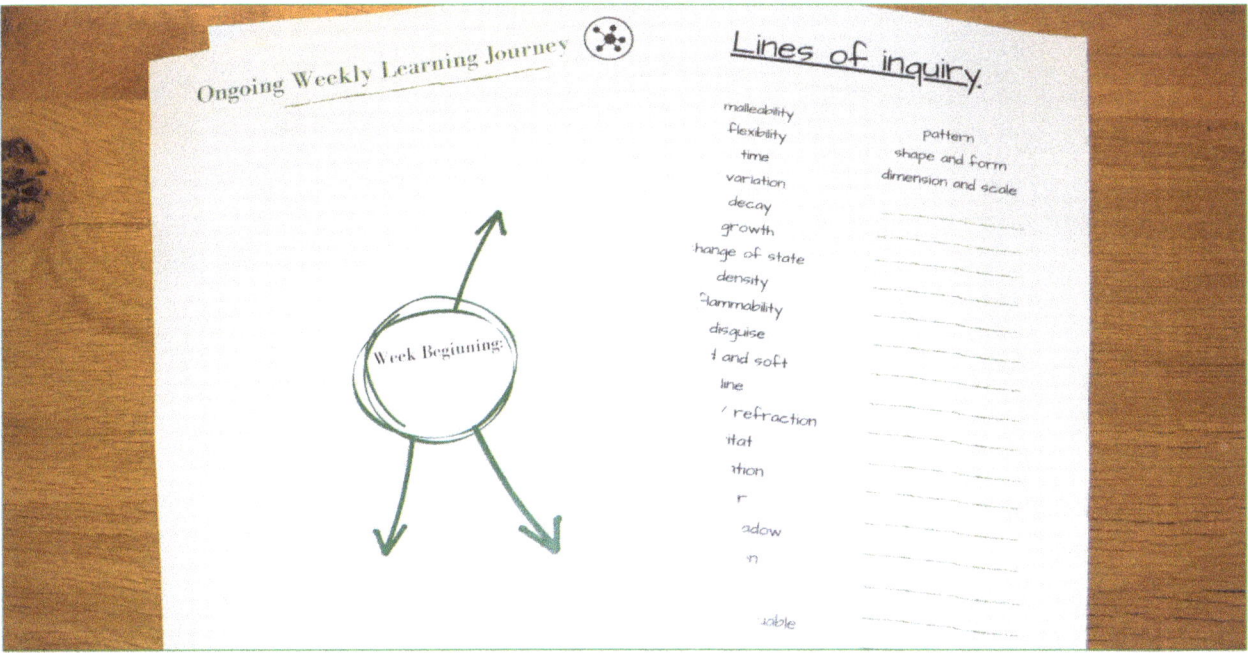

Active observation

To understand active observation, we need to be able to develop the skill of seeing and then understanding what we see. This will require more than one perspective; educators can view the same moment in many different ways and embracing this diverse range of views makes the professional dialogue richer.

This means that when we observe a child building with bricks, we don't reduce it to 'they are building with bricks' but instead notice the detail. That is why it is an active observation: the educators need to focus, to tune in to what children are fascinated by. Was it the form of the brick in their hand, the movement as it started to slide on the other brick, or the weight? Recording these aspects in a notebook, the Floorbook or a planning diary supports our planning to be detailed and rich. Conversations as a team about what we observe, using the Floorbook to revisit children's voices, their ideas and plans alongside film and imagery, give us the opportunity to base our planning on reality rather than on adult-created activities.

> What do you notice about how the children are sharing what they know?
>
> Are they revisiting an idea or demonstrating a fascination with something?

Lines of inquiry

The myriad of conversations that take place in a group of children all have value and purpose but sometimes as the educator we can identify an underlying line of inquiry. This is a fascination that persists over time and becomes a central idea that is explored in many ways through the duration of the inquiry.

The line of inquiry or central idea has some characteristics that support us to understand whether we have reached it.

- The central idea is written in one phrase or sentence – eg, 'the movement of grass, feathers and leaves', 'change', 'linearity'.
- It expresses concisely an enduring understanding – eg, the inquiry explored a link between mass and movement.
- It is substantial enough to generate in-depth inquiries. For example, 'movement and dimensions' is broad enough for depth but not as wide as the whole of movement.
- An effective line of inquiry is often concept-driven.

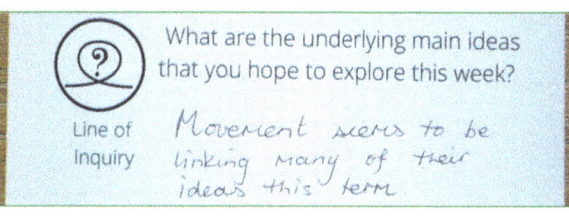

91

- It promotes the ability to think critically.
- It challenges and extends children's prior knowledge by taking their thinking as the starting point.
- A line of inquiry is a means of extending children's understanding of relationships across areas of learning.
- It is transferable across all children.
- It is relevant, engaging and significant.
- It allows for action to be taken in a way that makes sense to children.

> What is the underlying concept, knowledge or skill that the children are exploring?
>
> How have you decided on a main idea to explore?
>
> Is it broad enough to support the many ideas and fascinations of your children?

Possible lines of development

A possible line of development is written following an observation, a little like a 'next step', but is clearly linked to the larger lines of inquiry. PLODs are taken directly from the Floorbook when they are going to be completed. The documentation of these would then go back into the Floorbook.

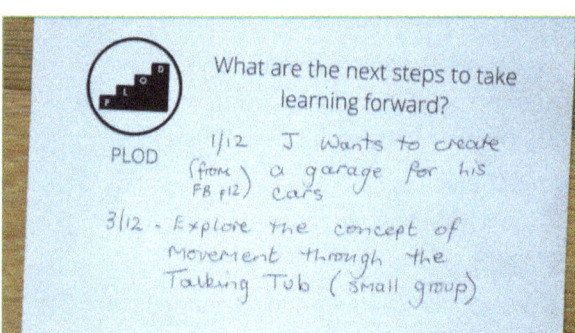

If we note a next step is to 'put out crayons', it doesn't convey why the experience or opportunity is taking place. It could be that it links to an outcome in the curriculum or a broader concept. So a clearer approach could be:

> 'Offer a range of materials to explore the difference between wax crayons and chalk.' or
>
> 'Offer crayons to investigate properties of materials.'

These examples give a clear message to the adults of what may emerge when they engage in dialogue. The actual resources may be the same but the intent, and therefore the interaction by the adult, may be richer and more connected to the child's inquiry. In summary, a PLOD consists of two parts:

> 'Offer this … in order to explore this …'

There are many ways of developing what children are exploring in play-based pedagogies; primarily through what they say, do, make or write. In the early stages of primary education, as the process of inquiry is under pressure to move from something freer to becoming more guided by invitations, we can use these columns to give children the choice of how they share their ideas. They can do so in either the group Floorbook or individual Learning Journals over the year to give them a wide range of opportunities. Blank sections at the end of both documents provide space for children to add their ideas, making it possible to monitor that children are experiencing a range of opportunities to share what they know.

> How could we offer new opportunities that take forward an idea?
>
> To what extent do the children in the early stages (3–7 years) engage in the opportunities in Table 4.1?
>
> How do we monitor that the ideas of the children and the ideas of the adult were balanced?

SECTION 4. BREADTH, BALANCE AND ACCOUNTABILITY

Table 4.1: Sharing multiple ways of knowing through say, do, make and write

Say	Do	Make	Write
Describe a model	Role play	Model	Leaflet
Explain a process	Explore materials	Pictures	Poem
Share ideas	Dance	Book	Letter
Talk to a friend	Sing	Map	Newspaper
Group discussion	Draw	Collage	Song
Questions	Play a game	Game	Report
Agree targets	Design	Mask	List
Hot seating	Record a song	Song	Menu
Circle time	Experiment	Rhyme	Thinking bubble
Pretend TV	Puppet show	Puppet	Invitations
Newsreader	Go for walk	Diagram	2D mind map
Directions	Set up a display	Quiz	Mini books
Instructions	Research	Animation	Envelopes
Recall	Investigate	Cartoon	Postcards
Show and tell	Look outside	Storyboard	Signs
Talkaround Time	Sit outside	Draw	Labels
Talking Tub	Walk and think	Recipe	Story
Song	Take photos	Advertisement	Play
Poem	Revisit the Floorbook	Food	Summary
Facts	Read personal profile	Structure	Email
Podcast	Share Family Book	Sculpture	Blog
Debate	3D mind map	Painting	Booklet
Story	Talk about a model	Create an image:	Diary
Talk about the failures	Slideshow	• with clay/dough	Thinking Tree leaf
Discuss: Think, pair and share	Puzzle/jigsaw	• with or in sand	A fact list
	Play with loose parts inside	• with loose natural materials	A detailed diagram or drawing
	Play outside		Plan
			Draw a model
			Recipe

SECTION 4. BREADTH, BALANCE AND ACCOUNTABILITY

Form of documentation

To document children's thinking is to capture the traces of play, the processes that are in constant movement. Documentation is therefore complex and the mere process of transferring what we see children do into an understanding is going to be inaccurate. However, the closer we pay attention, the more authentic the result.

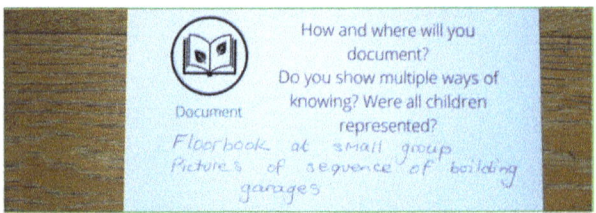

Allowing ourselves to document what we really see, as opposed to what we want to see, is a real challenge. Carla Rinaldi (2006) suggests that documentation is:

> visible listening, as the construction of traces (through notes, slides, videos and so on) that not only testify to the children's learning paths and processes, but also make them possible because they are visible. For us, this means making visible, and thus possible, the relationships that are the building blocks of knowledge. (p 68)

In this complexity, we use the Floorbooks to hold the multiple perspectives of what we think we see as the adults so that each day we can gather deeper and more accurate records, leading to a deeper understanding of the children's thinking.

> What aspects of what you see are significant?
>
> How can you involve children in their documentation?

Engaging children

The younger the child, the more intuitive and responsive the adult needs to be as the child responds to the world around them. All children deserve to be with adults who consider how they will offer an experience or an opportunity. One of the reasons for our choice of a Talking Tub was driven by a group of children many years ago who loved boxes and the thrill of opening them.

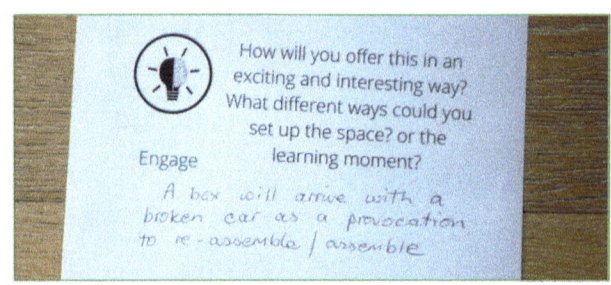

In this area of the planning diary, it is important that the adult considers what will frame the moment. Will it be inside or outside? Will the resources be put on display or will the children collect them? How long do you think children may be engaged for? Will there be a provocation or an invitation set up?

Provocations often:

- are based on children's own wonderings
- expand or extend children's own ideas, interest and theories
- deepen children's unique thinking
- provide new experiences and outcomes within their own sphere of interest and are related to their existing thinking.

Invitations often:

- are based on teacher wonderings and thoughts
- give an idea or a reason for doing something
- spark children's motivation and interest when well framed
- offer new possibilities and wider awareness for children.

> How will you offer an invitation to engage in your intentional experience?
>
> How do you empower children to take the lead?
>
> Are the provocations you use beautiful? Challenging? Relevant?

Focus to be intentional

The main focus of your planning should be on improving the quality of provision for the child. To do this, we need to be aware of the small things that make a difference. Any intentional experience will contain many possibilities and interpretations. The focus of the planning diary here

SECTION 4. BREADTH, BALANCE AND ACCOUNTABILITY

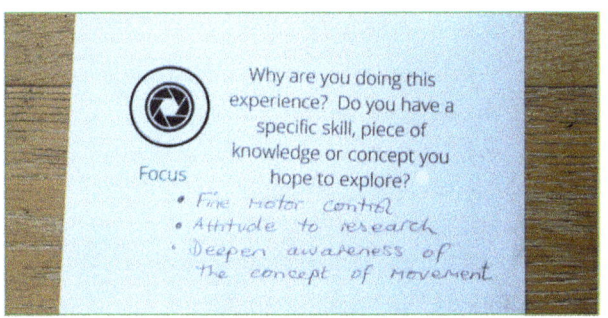
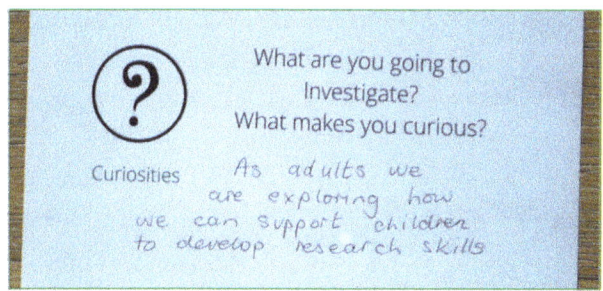

is to pick up on whether your practice is actually looking in detail to notice a skill that needs to be developed or a piece of knowledge that a child wants to share, or indeed for the adult to highlight a concept or introduce some vocabulary. Having a focus or clear intent to your planning, based on your knowledge of the children you work with, is effective in supporting progression.

By looking through the Floorbook to assess engagement and understanding, it is possible to understand how the dynamic of your group of children responds to your intentional planning and what kind of experience they enjoy and seem to respond to.

> When you plan for an experience, what is its underlying focus?
>
> How do you leave enough space in these invitations for children to lead the direction of their own learning?

Investigations and inquiries

Inquiry never stops; the learning journey could weave itself together over several years. However, we traditionally view experiences in blocks and here it is valuable to note questions that arose that were not necessarily part of the main inquiry but that would have real value if picked up in the future. This can be done with an individual fascination, such as looking up the answer to why beetles have wings, or indeed the larger group might explore flight and wings more broadly. By going back through the planning diary at the end of term, the educator can note down what fascinations children have to inform future planning.

> What kinds of things seem to fascinate your children?
>
> Is there value in exploring it now? Could you revisit it later?

Connections and links

Children are part of a physical and cultural community, so it supports them when the educator can make links clear. It could be that the children are exploring bees and someone mentions that their uncle has some. This links to relationships; inviting those people in to share in the learning journey can make that journey richer and more meaningful.

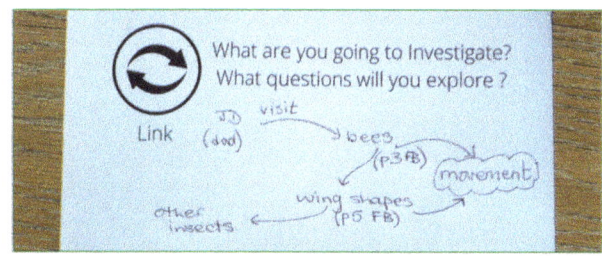

Family voices

Children are competent and capable and hold memories that can be easily triggered through an image or a conversation. The link may seem abstract at first but, as the conversation develops, a connection from the child's lived experience to the dialogue may become clear. For example, a child was engaged in a conversation about a dog and in response they talked about a car. The connection turned out to be that the family dog was taken to the vet in a car. By noting down the links to follow up or conversations that came out of the Floorbook, the whole team can be aware of events to follow.

> How does the experience link to the real world to offer children a tangible understanding of the world around them?
>
> What links could you make in your interaction to previous experiences or events in the community?

Reflection

The symbol for this section indicates the question of self-reflection. To self-reflect effectively, we must be professionally honest and brave as it centres on why we do what we do. Where there are guiding principles or pedagogical values that we support, these are the backbone of our reflection.

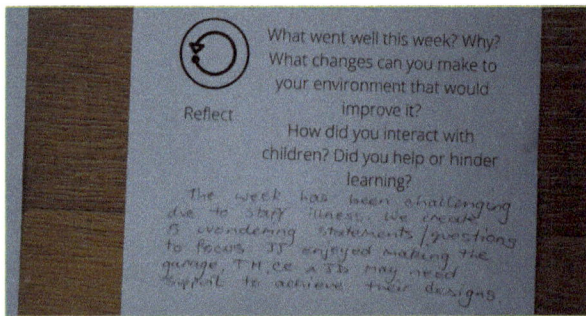

The reflections are in the planning cycle to support educators to embrace any changes to what they do, say or believe to improve the outcomes for children and families.

> How did you feel your interaction supported children?
>
> Was the experience meaningful, joyful and without bias?
>
> How could you have used the space, time and resources more effectively?
>
> What key things did you notice to take forward?

The learning journey

Floorbooks are a motivational way to document children's theories and ideas. These ideas can then be used as the basis for planning authentic and engaging experiences for children in a variety of settings. We need to be accountable. The key questions for me are: accountable to whom and why?

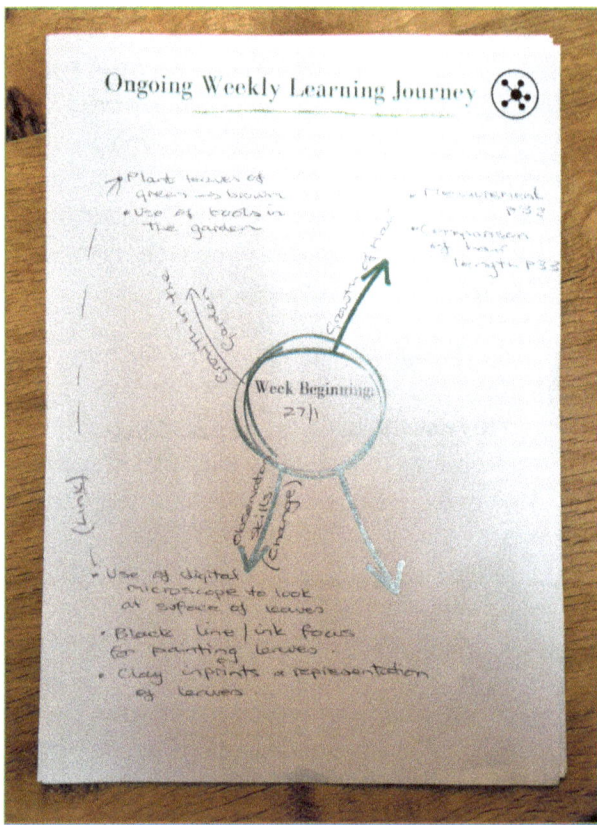

As an educator, I hold myself accountable first to children, and then to parents and families. Sometimes we can feel that we are accountable to outside agencies more than we are to the young children and families in our settings and schools. As professionals, we strive for quality and the accountability to larger agendas presented through care standards, or balanced curriculum experiences and outcomes, should be seen in a positive way when that process of accountability keeps children at the heart. Curricula sit around the world to monitor the breadth and balance of experiences. They evolve and respond to their social setting and time period. The elements that change are within the content of the curriculum and the methodology of delivery.

SECTION 4. BREADTH, BALANCE AND ACCOUNTABILITY

The pedagogy (study of how to teach) of environments that use Floorbooks embraces the child as competent and skilled, follows a listening pedagogy that includes and respects all voices and ensures that learning journeys flow and move across time and space boundaries to make connections and links for children.

> How long has the learning journey taken?
>
> How did you show the links and connections to the evidence? Did you include page numbers?

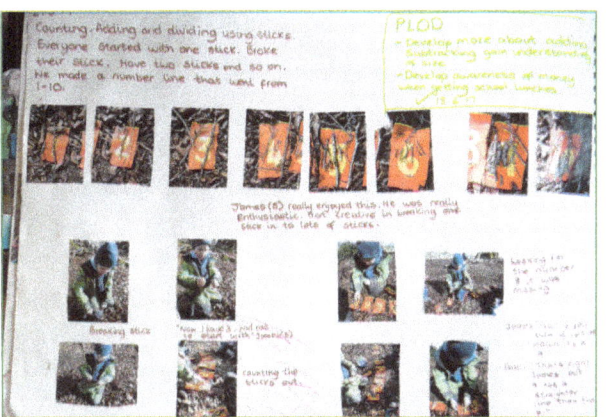

Sharing learning outside

Looking through a Floorbook

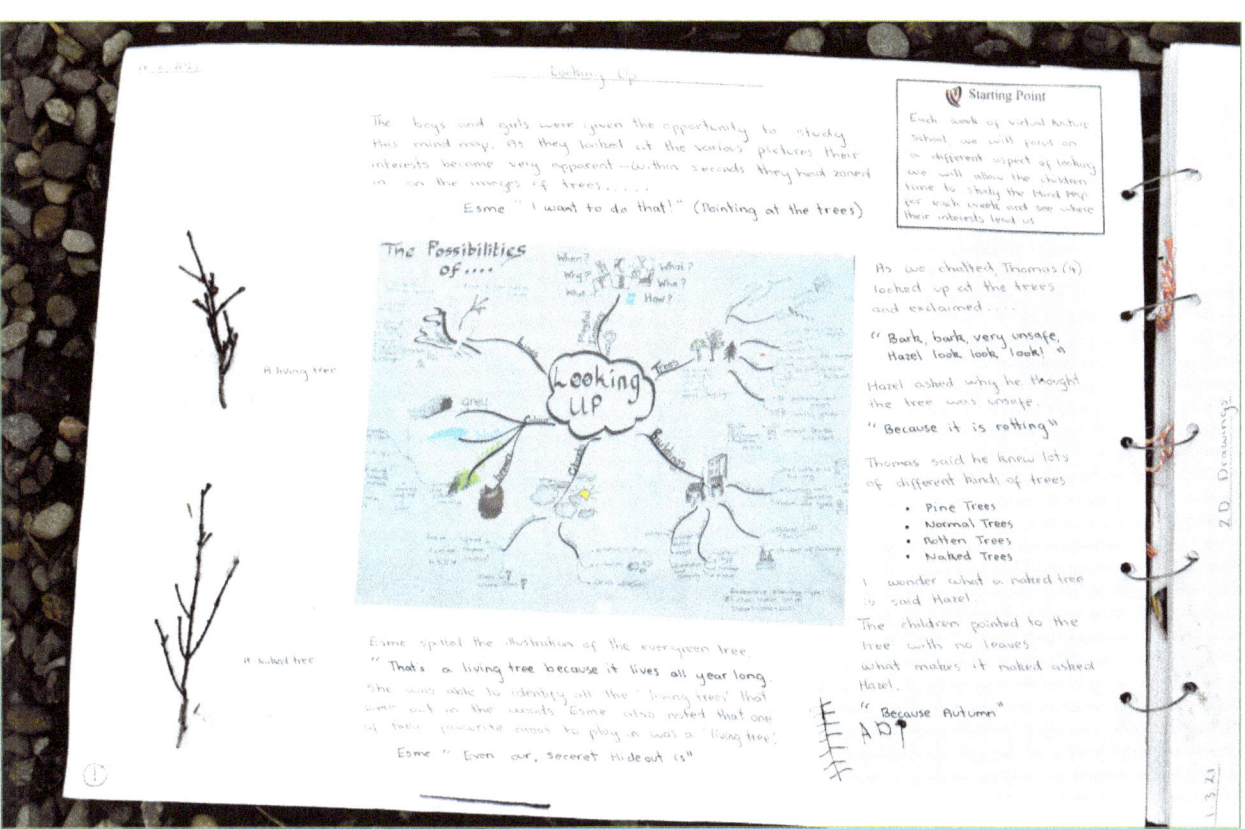

The learning journey as a provocation for another group of children

Conclusion

Through this book we have explored the need for planning with and for children as something bigger than a requirement: it is a way of being, a consultative pedagogy that supports confident and capable children to flourish in education and care rather than be bound by it. After years of research around the globe, the most effective strategies have crystallised so that they are now at your fingertips to support your interaction with children, families and community. The approach to planning outlined in Section 4 provides practical guidance on how to make the paperwork you do have a positive impact, so that assessment informs what you do every day.

Children have a constant, high-speed exposure to experiences and an associated high rate at which we expect them to retain and recall knowledge. It is not sustainable as a pedagogy. Moreover, some would argue that creating a method of working with children that is not relationship-focussed will be one of the greatest errors in education in our time.

The experience of a global pandemic has prompted people to revisit what really matters in the lives of children, which includes the need to be loved, active, enthused, heard, involved and supported to learn. These aspects are all covered by the inquiry-based approach that is central to the Floorbook Approach. Its strategies of using Talking Tubs, Talking and Thinking Trees and Talkaround Times allow adults and children to explore ideas as a learning community and co-construct a learning journey that may last a lifetime. When we use these strategies to assess and document those ideas and then take the plans and ideas forward into a diary, the planning cycle is complete. Planning with and for children achieves the goal of being child-led in our practice while maintaining accountability to documents such as the curriculum.

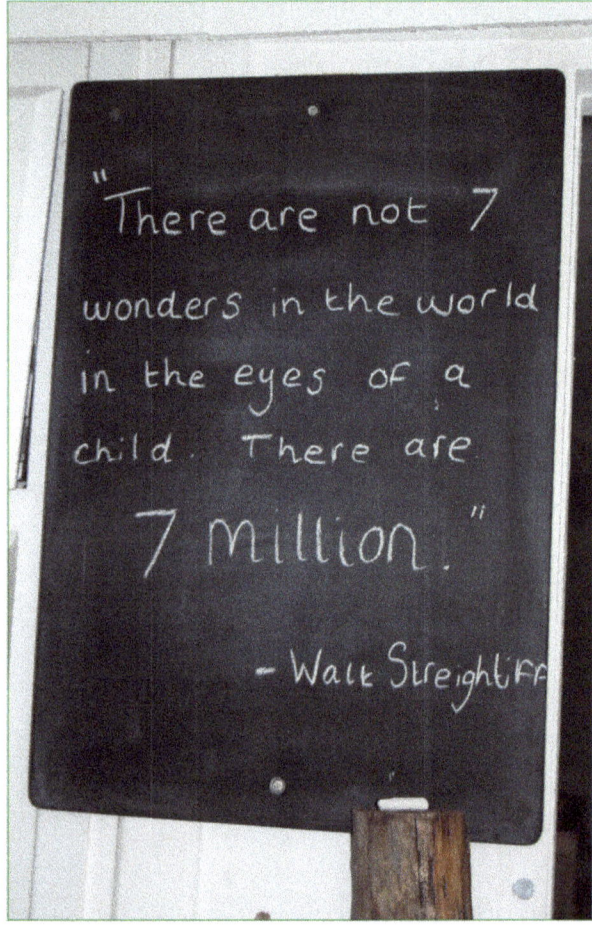

Adult documentation to inspire each other

Books made by children and adults together

References and further reading

Abbott, C and Godinho, S (2001) *Thinking Voices: Developing oral communication skills*. Carlton: Curriculum Corporation.

Adair, J, Colegrove, KS and McManus, M (2017) How the word gap argument negatively impacts young children of Latinx immigrants' conceptualizations of learning. *Harvard Educational Review* 87(3): 309–334.

Adlam, F (2018) *Raise Your Child to Read and Write: A guide for New Zealand parents: from birth to seven years*. Nelson: Potton & Burton.

Alexander, R (2008) *Towards Dialogic Teaching: Rethinking classroom talk* (4th edn). York: Dialogos UK.

Alexander, R (2012) Improving oracy and classroom talk in English schools: achievements and challenges. Presentation at the Department for Education Seminar on Oracy, the National Curriculum and Educational Standards, London.

Badakar, CM, Thakkar, PJ, Hugar, SM, Kukreja, P, Assudani, HG and Gokhale, N (2017) Evaluation of the relevance of Piaget's cognitive principles among parented and orphan children in Belagavi City, Karnataka, India: a comparative study. *International Journal of Clinical Pediatric Dentistry* 10(4): 346–350. doi: 10.5005/jp-journals-10005-1463

Beetlestone, F (1998) *Creative Children, Imaginative Teaching*. Buckingham: Open University Press.

Bentley, T (1998) *Learning Beyond the Classroom*. London and New York: Routledge.

Blackwell, CK, Lauricella, AR and Wartella, E (2014) Factors influencing digital technology use in early childhood education. *Computers & Education* 77: 82–90.

Board of Studies NSW (2005). *NSW Primary Curriculum Foundation Statements*.

Bruce, T (2004) *Cultivating Creativity in Babies, Toddlers and Young Children*. London: Hodder and Stoughton Educational.

Bruner, JS (1961) The act of discovery. *Harvard Educational Review* 31: 21–32.

Bruner, JS (1996) *The Culture of Education*. Cambridge, MA: Harvard University Press.

Bruner, JS, Goodnow, JJ and Austin, G (1986) *A Study of Thinking*. New York, NY: Routledge.

Burnard, P, Craft, A and Grainger, T (2006) Possibility thinking. *International Journal of Early Years Education* 14(3): 243–262.

Cantone, KF (2007) *Code-switching in Bilingual Children*. Dordrecht: Springer.

Caputo, JD (1987) *Radical Hermeneutics: Repetition, deconstruction, and the hermeneutic project*. Bloomington, IN: University of Indiana Press.

Carr, M (2000) *Assessment in Early Childhood Settings: Learning stories*. London: Sage.

Carr, M (2006) Learning dispositions and key competencies: a new curriculum continuity across the sectors? *Set* (2).

Carr, M and Lee, W (2012) *Learning Stories: Constructing earner identities in early education*. London: Sage.

Chancellor, B (2008) *Analysis of Curriculum/Learning Frameworks for the Early Years (Birth to Age 8)*. Melbourne: Victorian Curriculum and Assessment Authority.

Clark, A and Moss, P (2005) *Listening to Young Children: The mosaic approach*. London: NCB.

Claxton, G (2002) *Building Learning Power*. Bristol: TLO.

Claxton, G and Carr, M (2004) A framework for teaching learning: the dynamics of disposition. *Early Years: An international research journal* 24(1): 87–97.

Coşkun, H and Durakoğlu, A (2015) A project-based approach in child education: Reggio Emilia. *International Journal of Humanities and Education* 1(2): 141–153.

Costa, A and Kallick, B (2000) *Discovering and Exploring Habits of Mind*. Alexandria, VA: ASCD.

Craft, A (1999) Creative development in the early years: some implications of policy for practice. *The Curriculum Journal*, 10(1): 135–150.

Craft, A (2000) *Creativity across the Primary Curriculum*. London: Routledge.

Craft, A (2001) Little c Creativity. In A Craft, B Jeffrey and M Leibling (eds) *Creativity in Education*. London: Continuum, pp 45–61.

Craft, A (2002) *Creativity and Early Years Education*. London: Continuum.

References and further reading

Cremin, T, Burnard, P and Craft, A (2006) Pedagogy and possibility thinking in the early years. *International Journal of Thinking Skills and Creativity* 1(2): 108–119.

Denham, SA (1986) Social cognition, prosocial behaviour and emotion in pre-schoolers: contextual validation. *Child Development* 57: 194–201.

Department for Education, England (2025) *Early Years Foundation Stage Statutory Framework: For group and school-based providers: Setting the standards for learning, development and care for children from birth to five (England)*. URL: gov.uk/government/publications/early-years-foundation-stage-framework--2 (accessed 12 September 2025).

Department for Education, England (no date) Curriculum planning. URL: https://help-for-early-years-providers.education.gov.uk/support-for-practitioners/curriculum-planning (accessed 16 September 2025).

Duffy, B (2006) *Supporting Creativity and Imagination in the Early Years* (2nd edn). Maidenhead: Open University Press.

Dweck, CS (2006) *Mindset: The new psychology of success*. New York, NY: Random House.

Early Years Wales (2020) Foundation learning. URL: www.earlyyears.wales/en/foundation-phase (accessed 16 September 2025).

Eaude, T (2011) *Thinking through Pedagogy for Primary and Early Years*. London: Sage.

Education Scotland (2016) *How Good is our Early Learning and Childcare?* Livingston: Education Scotland. URL: https://education.gov.scot/inspection-and-review/inspection-frameworks/how-good-is-our-early-learning-and-childcare/ (accessed 12 September 2025).

Education Scotland (2019) *Curriculum for Excellence (refreshed edition)*. URL: https://scotlandscurriculum.scot (accessed 29 September 2025).

Education Scotland. (2020) *Realising the Ambition – Being Me: National practice guidance for early years in Scotland*. Livingston: Education Scotland. URL: https://education.gov.scot/media/3bjpr3wa/realisingtheambition.pdf (accessed 12 September 2025).

Education Scotland and Care Inspectorate (2025) *A Quality Improvement Framework for the Early Learning and Childcare Sectors*. URL: https://education.gov.scot/inspection-and-review/inspection-frameworks/quality-improvement-framework-for-the-early-learning-and-childcare-sectors/early-learning-and-childcare-quality-indicators/ (accessed 29 September 2025).

Eisenberg, AR (1999) Emotion talk among Mexican-American and Anglo-American mothers and children from two social classes. *Merrill-Palmer Quarterly* 45(2): 267–284.

Erickson, HL and Lanning L (2013) *Transitioning to Concept-based Curriculum and Instruction: How to bring content and process together*. Thousand Oaks, CA: Corwin.

Farida, N and Rasyid, H (2018) Effectiveness of project based learning approach to social development of early childhood. *Advances in Social Science, Education and Humanities Research* 296: 369–372.

Feldman, RS, McGee, G, Mann, L and Strain, PS (1993) Nonverbal affective decoding ability in children with autism and in typical pre-schoolers. *Journal of Early Intervention* 17 (4): 341–350.

Fleet, A, Patterson, C and Robertson, J (2017) *Pedagogical Documentation in Early Years Practice: Seeing through multiple perspectives*. Thousand Oaks, CA: Sage.

French, R and Marschall, C (2016) *Concept-based Inquiry in Action: Strategies to promote transferable understanding*. Thousand Oaks, CA: Corwin Teaching Essentials.

Gander, K (2019, 25 March) Parents and toddlers interact more when reading paper books versus e-books. *Newsweek*.

Gandini, L (1993) Fundamentals of the Reggio Emilia approach to early childhood education. *Young Children* 49(1): 4–8.

Gardner, H (1993) *Multiple Intelligences: The theory in practice*. New York, NY: Basic Books.

Gilkerson, J, Richards, JA, Warren, SF, Montgomery, JK, Greenwood, CR, Kimbrough Oller, D, Hansen, J and Paul, TD (2017) Mapping the early language environment using all-day recordings and automated analysis. *American Journal of Speech-language Pathology* 26(2): 248–265. doi: 10.1044/2016_AJSLP-15-0169

Golding, C (2002) *Connecting Concepts: Thinking activities for students*. Melbourne: ACER Press.

Goouch, K (2008) Understanding playful pedagogies, play narratives and play spaces. *Early Years: An International Research Journal* 28(1): 93–102.

Hall, K, Horgan, M, Ridgway, A, Murphy, R, Cunneen, M and Cunningham, D (eds) (2010) *Loris Malaguzzi and the Reggio Emilia Experience*. New York, NY: Continuum.

Hart, L (1983) *Human Brain and Human Learning*. Oak Creek: AZ Books for Educators

References and Further Reading

Helm, JH and Beneke, S (2003) *The Power of Projects: Meeting contemporary challenges in early childhood classrooms – strategies and solutions*. New York, NY: Teachers College Press.

Helm, JH and Katz, L (2001) *Young Investigators: The project approach in the early years*. New York, NY: Teachers College Press.

Helm, JH, Beneke, S, and Steinheimer, K (2007) *Windows on Learning: Documenting young children's work*. New York, NY: Teachers College Press.

Howard, P (2006) *The Owner's Manual for the Brain: Everyday applications from mind-brain research*. Austin, TX: Bard Press.

Jeffrey, B (2004) End-of-Award Report: Creative Learning and Student Perspectives (CLASP) Project. Submitted to Economic and Social Research Council.

Jeffrey, B (2005) Final Report of the Creative Learning and Student Perspectives Research Project (CLASP). A European Commission Funded project through the Socrates Programme, Action 6.1, Number 2002 – 4682 / 002 – 001. SO2 – 61OBGE. Milton Keynes.

Jeffrey, B and Craft, A (2004) Teaching creatively and teaching for creativity: distinctions and relationships. *Educational Studies* 30(1): 77–87.

Jeffrey, B and Woods, P (2003) *The Creative School: A framework for success, quality and effectiveness*. London: Routledge Falmer.

Jeffrey, G (2001) Primary pupils' perspectives and creative learning. *Encyclopaedia* 9: 133–152 (Italian journal).

Jeffrey, G (ed) (2005) *The Creative College: Building a successful learning culture in the arts*. Stoke-on-Trent: Trentham Books.

Joseph, GE and Strain, PS (2003) Enhancing emotional vocabulary in young children. *Young Exceptional Children* 6(4): 18–26.

Kotulak, R (1993) Unlocking the mind. *Chicago Tribune*.

Kuhn, S and Davidson, J (2007) Thinking with things, teaching with things. *Qualitative Research Journal* 7(2): 63–75.

Laevers, F (1993) Deep level learning: an exemplary application on the area of physical knowledge. *European Early Childhood Education Research Journal* 1(1): 53–68.

Leggo, C (2007) Scribbled subjects. *Journal of the Canadian Association for Curriculum Studies* 5(1): 31.

Lemke, JL (2000) Across the scales of time: artifacts, activities, and meanings in ecosocial systems. *Mind, Culture and Activity* 7(4): 273–290.

Lipman, M (1988) Critical thinking: what can it be? *Educational Leadership* 46(1): 38–43.

Livingston, K, Schweisfurth, M, Brace, G and Nash, M (2017) *Why Pedagogy Matters: The role of pedagogy in education 2030: A policy paper*. Education 2030 Framework for Action.

Malaguzzi, L (1993) History, ideas, and basic philosophy. In C Edwards, L Gandini and G Forman (eds) *The Hundred Languages of Children: The Reggio Emilia approach to early childhood education*. Norwood, NJ: Ablex.

Mitchell, S, Foulger, TS, Wetzel, K and Rathkey, C (2009) The negotiated project approach: project-based learning without leaving the standards behind. *Early Childhood Education Journal* 36(4): 339.

Morss, JR (1996) *Growing Critical: Alternatives to developmental psychology*. New York, NY: Routledge.

Ng, AK (2003) A cultural model of creative and conforming behaviour. *Creativity Research Journal* 15(2–3): 223–233.

Papert, S (1993) *The Children's Machine: Rethinking schools in the age of the computer*. New York, NY: Basic Books.

Pascal, C and Bertram, A (eds) (1997) *Effective Early Learning: Case studies of improvement*. London: Hodder and Stoughton.

Pellegrini, AD (2009) *The Role of Play in Human Development*. New York: Oxford University Press.

Piaget, J (1977) *The Essential Piaget*. Edited by HE Gruber and JJ Voneche. New York, NY: Basic Books.

Pitri, E (2004) Situated learning in a classroom community. *Art Education* 57(6): 6–12.

Rinaldi, C (2006) *In Dialogue with Reggio Emelia: Listening, researching and learning*. New York, NY: Routledge.

Rogoff, B (2003) *The Cultural Nature of Human Development*. Oxford and New York: Oxford University Press.

Schaffer, R (1996) *Social Development*. Oxford: Blackwell.

Schon, D (1987) *Educating the Reflective Practitioner*. San Francisco, CA: Jossey-Bass.

Scott, HK (2019). Piaget. StatPearls [Internet].

REFERENCES AND FURTHER READING

Scottish Government (2017) Health and Social Care standards: My support, my life. URL: www.gov.scot/publications/health-social-care-standards-support-life/ (accessed 16 September 2025).

Seltzer, K and Bentley, T (1999) *The Creative Age: Knowledge and skills for the new economy.* London: Demos.

Siraj-Blatchford, I and Manni, L (2008) 'Would you like to tidy up now?' An analysis of adult questioning in the English Foundation Stage. *Early Years: An international journal of research and development* 28(1): 5–22.

Smidt, S (2013) *Introducing Malaguzzi.* London and New York: Routledge.

Smith, SR (ed) (2007) *Applying Theory to Practice: Issues for critical reflection.* Aldershot: Ashgate.

Sorin, R and Galloway, G (2006) Constructs of childhood: constructs of self. *Children Australia* 31(2): 12–21.

Sylva, K (2004) The Effective Provision of Preschool Education (EPPE) Project. Presentation at British Educational Research Association Annual Conference, University of Manchester. UK.

Sylva, K Sammons, P, Melhuish, E, Siraj-Blatchford, I and Taggart, B (1999) The Effective Provision of Pre-School Education (EPPE) Project: Technical Paper 1 – an introduction to the EPPE Project. London: DfEe / Institute of Education, University of London.

Sylwester, R (1995) *A Celebration of Neurons: An educator's guide to the human brain.* Alexandria, VA: Association for Supervision and Curriculum Development.

Sylwester, R (2004) *How to Explain a Brain: An educator's handbook of brain terms and cognitive processes.* Thousand Oaks, CA: Corwin Press.

Timperley, H, Kaser, L and Halbert, J (2014) *A Framework for Transforming Learning in Schools: Innovation and the spiral of inquiry.* Centre for Strategic Education, Seminar Series Paper No. 234.

von Stumm, S, Hell, B and Chamorro-Premuzic, T (2011) The hungry mind: intellectual curiosity is the third pillar of academic performance. *Perspectives on Psychological Science* 6(6): 574. doi: 10.1177/1745691611421204

Vygotsky, LS (1978) *Mind in Society.* Cambridge, MA: Harvard University Press.

Wagner, F (2014) Presentation at summer school, Institut Camille Jordan, Lyon University, France.

Warden, C (1996) *Talking and Thinking Floorbooks.* Scotland: Mindstretchers.

Warden, C (2015) *Learning with Nature: Embedding outdoor practice.* London: Sage.

Warden, C (2018) The Creation and Theorisation of a Nature Pedagogy. Unpublished PhD thesis, University of Liverpool, United Kingdom.

Webster-Stratton, C (1999) *How to Promote Children's Social and Emotional Competence.* London: Paul Chapman.

Welsh Government (2024) *Curriculum for Wales.* URL: https://hwb.gov.wales/curriculum-for-wales/ (accessed 29 September 2025).

Wertsch, J (1998) *Mind as Action.* Oxford: Oxford University Press.

White, BL, Kahan, J and Attanucci, JS (1979) *The Origins of Human Competence.* Lexington, MA: Lexington Books.

Whitehurst, G and Lonigan, C (2001) *Emergent Literacy: Development from prereaders to readers.* New York, NY: Guilford Press.

Wiebe, S, Sameshima, P, Irwin, R, Leggo, C, Gouzouasis, P and Grauer, K (2007) Re-imagining arts integration: rhizomatic relations of the everyday. *Journal of Educational Thought (JET) / Revue de la Pensée Éducative* 41(3): 263–280.

Wilks, S (1995) *Critical and Creative Thinking.* Portsmouth, NH: Heinemann.

Wolfe, P (2001) *Brain Matters: Translating research into classroom practice.* Alexandria, VA: ASCD.

Zull, J (2002) *The Art of Changing the Brain: Enriching the practice of teaching by exploring the biology of learning.* Sterling, VA: Stylus.

Glossary

Child-led planning and documentation	A form of planning that shares the responsibility of decision-making between the child and the adult. The adult observes and listens to children's ideas, analyses them, considers the connections and then offers an opportunity to extend the learning.
Co-constructivist approach	An approach that views knowledge as constructed between two people. It suggests that learning is primarily a social activity.
Communication Book	The Communication Book is a centralised record of the many and varied ways that we communicate with the setting's wider community such as visitors, parents and local members of the community. The Communication Book helps to link families into the Floorbook Approach. It provides an effective informal way of supporting parental engagement at your setting as visitors and parents write messages, thoughts and feedback in it.
Family Book	Part of the Floorbook Approach, the Family Book is A4 size and used to create interesting, relevant, accessible and individual profiles for children that are built on stories and experiences with the family and in the setting. It supports child-led documentation and gives each child a voice that can then be easily shared with their family.
Floorbook	The central hub of documentation in the Floorbook Approach, which connects many forms of observation and assessment of children's thinking. It is usually shared in an A2 book to give groups of children space to work together. The Floorbook shares the many forms of communication that arise from inquiry-based learning to support child-led planning and documentation. Floorbooks share ideas, reflections, challenges, solutions and failures, thoughts, actions, observations, plans and desires. They also allow children to revisit their learning as often as they wish, meaning that they can also reflect on earlier learning in relation to what they have learnt since.
Floorbook Approach	Dr Claire Warden created the Floorbook Approach in 1986 to give the educator strategies to truly consult with children during the planning and documentation process. The approach supports inquiry-based learning, develops higher-order thinking skills and helps children influence their own learning journey. This innovative child-led approach to observation, documentation and planning is now implemented in settings around the world. By listening to children and identifying their interests, we can create a unique learning opportunity that excites and interests them.
Formative assessment	A continual form of assessment that informs day-to-day practice.
Implicit curriculum	In contrast to the core curriculum, which can be made visible through experiences or outcomes, the implicit curriculum is not obvious. It focuses on the aspects of the curriculum that are concerned with values and beliefs.

continued ...

GLOSSARY

Inquiry-based learning	Inquiry-based learning is integral to the Floorbook Approach. It goes further than asking a child what they want to know to trigger curiosity and fascination. Inquiry-based learning is a form of active learning that starts by asking open-ended questions or provocations. The response to these provocations takes the group on a learning journey over many weeks and months. There are many types of inquiry-based approaches.
Line of inquiry	The main idea or concept that lies beneath an experience or opportunity. Using lines of inquiry to plan experiences supports children to make links in their play.
Mind map	Originally promoted by Tony Buzan, mind mapping uses graphics to help children see the relationship between their ideas. Mind maps can be 2D and written on paper or can follow the Floorbook Approach, where we use 3D objects and images, write main ideas on yellow strips of paper and write individual contributions in thinking bubbles.
PLOD	A 'possible line of development' or 'possible line of direction'. This two-part objective states what you are going to offer and what you hope children will explore. For example: (1) Provide a variety of containers in the water tray … (2) to explore capacity.
Summative assessment	A form of assessment that occurs at the end of a piece of work as a summary.
Talkaround Mat	The ritual of putting out the Talkaround Mat invites children to come together to share their thoughts and ideas. The mat is large (2 metres in diameter) and plain black to support children to visually engage with the objects or experience taking place. In this portable area, an educator can easily organise and encourage child-led discussions, which will create possible lines of development to include in the Floorbook and planning diary.
Talkaround Time	The time when children and educators gather in a group on the Talkaround Mat to explore a Talking Tub or look at a Floorbook together. It's a time when all children are encouraged to contribute their thoughts and feelings in a positive and supportive environment.
Talking and Thinking Trees	As an element of the Floorbook Approach, Talking and Thinking Trees are a fun way to engage children. The tree is used in conjunction with paper leaves to allow children to share their ideas, thoughts and learning and document the planning cycle in your setting.
Talking Tub	Talking Tubs support you to engage children in conversation and dialogue, which in turn will create possible lines of development for planning. Designed to support adult organisation, they hold a variety of real 2D and 3D objects that will promote oracy and richer thinking.
Thinking Bubbles	These are paper shapes cut to suggest thinking. They can support children who are concerned about writing as they are often made of recycled paper and represent freedom from the secretarial skills of writing. Children draw or write their ideas and thoughts on them and then use them to sort ideas or to create mind maps. Thinking Bubbles can later be stored in an envelope in the Floorbook to document learning.

www.ingramcontent.com/pod-product-compliance
Lightning Source LLC
Chambersburg PA
CBHW061539010526
44112CB00022B/2891